CAMPAIGN 401

JAMESTOWN 1622

The Anglo-Powhatan Wars

CAMERON COLBY   ILLUSTRATED BY MARCO CAPPARONI

OSPREY PUBLISHING
Bloomsbury Publishing Plc
Kemp House, Chawley Park, Cumnor Hill, Oxford OX2 9PH, UK
29 Earlsfort Terrace, Dublin 2, Ireland
1385 Broadway, 5th Floor, New York, NY 10018, USA
E-mail: info@ospreypublishing.com
www.ospreypublishing.com

OSPREY is a trademark of Osprey Publishing Ltd

First published in Great Britain in 2024

A catalog record for this book is available from the British Library.

ISBN: PB 9781472861924; eBook 9781472861931; ePDF 9781472861900;
XML 9781472861917

24 25 26 27 28   10 9 8 7 6 5 4 3 2 1

Maps by Bounford.com
3D BEV by Paul Kime
Index by Zoe Ross
Typeset by PDQ Digital Media Solutions, Bungay, UK
Printed and bound in India by Replika Press Private Ltd

To find out more about our authors and books visit
www.ospreypublishing.com. Here you will find extracts, author
interviews, details of forthcoming events and the option to sign up for
our newsletter.

Osprey Publishing supports the Woodland Trust, the UK's leading woodland
conservation charity.

Artist's note

Readers may care to note that the original paintings from which the colour
plates in this book were prepared are available for private sale. All
reproduction copyright whatsoever is retained by the publishers. All
enquiries should be addressed to the artist via the below website:

https://marcocapparoni.com/

The publishers regret that they can enter into no correspondence upon
this matter.

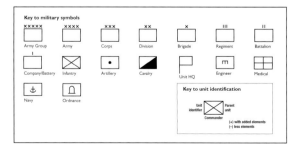

Front cover main illustration: The English attack on Pamunkey
villages of June 1624. (Marco Capparoni)

Title page photograph: A 1619 woodcut by Theodor de Bry
depicting Chief Japssus and Captain Argall conspiring to capture
Pocahontas. (Courtesy of the John Carter Brown Library)

CONTENTS

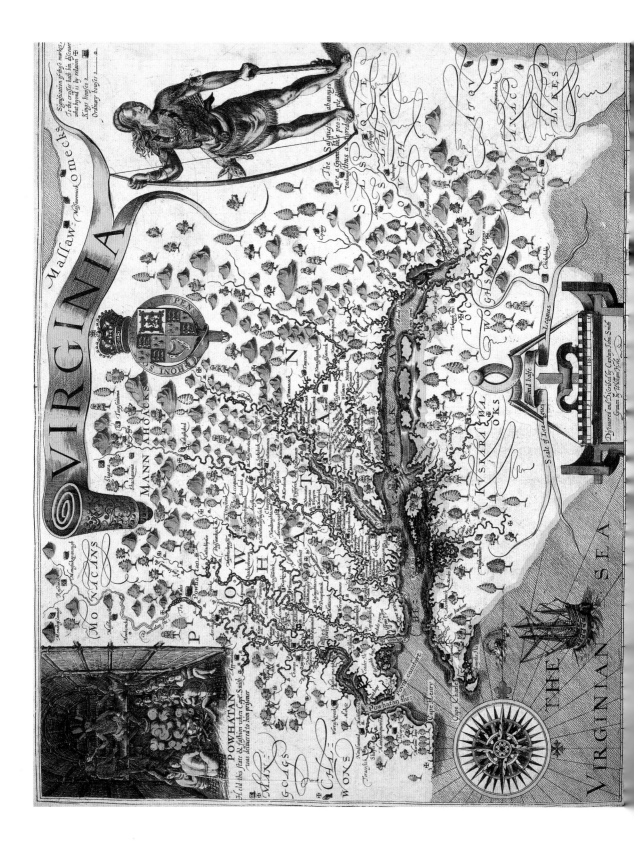

VIRGINIA

Massaw= Massawomecks omecks

The Sasquc= sahanougs are a Gyant like people portrayed thus a wildly

Signification of these markes To the croses hath bin discouer what beyond is by relation Kings houses 2 Ordinary houses 2

POWHATAN Held this state & fashion when Capt. Smith was deliuered to him prisoner

Discouered and Discribed by Captayn John Smith Grauen by William Hole

Scale of Leagues

THE VIRGINIAN SEA

ORIGINS OF THE CAMPAIGN

The Virginia colony began with dreams of gold and empire. By January 1622, the Jamestown colony, nestled in the fingers of the Chesapeake Bay, optimistically limped into the spring planting season hoping to see a year of high-yield tobacco returns. After 15 years of high mortality and weak profits, the small enduring bands of Englishmen would soon face the most dangerous assault on English presence in Virginia.

On March 22, 1622, 347 Englishmen died in a surprise attack led by Powhatan Chieftain Opechancanough. This attack marked the beginning of the Second Anglo-Powhatan War. This book focuses on the events of the first and second Anglo-Powhatan wars. These conflicts demonstrate how cyclical surprise attacks in Virginia developed into multi-year war campaigns lifting settlers from the lowest point of English colonization to a coordinated colonial policy for English stability. Strategies developed by the fledgling colony created a model for English presence in the New World. A revolving door of leaders shaped the early English settlement, each bringing experience from around the globe. The Powhatan tribes followed Chief Opechancanough for most conflicts against the colony. The progress and outcomes of the first through third Anglo-Powhatan wars shaped English colonization of the New World.

Under the Tudor monarchy, England began its colonial endeavors in the Old World but quickly sought ventures in the west. Englishmen first encountered Algonquian peoples in the 1580s during the failed Roanoke colonies. Learning from the disasters at Roanoke, Jamestown endured thanks to relentless supply voyages. English relationships with their Algonquian Powhatan neighbors rose and fell during the first four decades of the colony.

The history of English expansion into the New World set the stakes for the nascent Jamestown colony. The reign of Elizabeth I (1558–1603) saw English experimentation in trade, colonies, and companies. A generation of this experimentation culminated with King James I (1603–25) pursuing his ventures into the Caribbean and North America. After 15 years of trials, the indigenous people of Virginia pushed the English experiment to the brink of collapse in 1622. United for survival and resolute to keep the colony alive after 1622, English colonists at Jamestown changed their focus from haphazard growth to determined expansive colonization.

OPPOSITE

John Smith drew this map based on his notes and experiences from his three years in Jamestown. The map depicts an "Indian" world with one small English settlement. The black Maltese crosses represent the extent of Smith's exploration, today commemorated by the Captain John Smith Chesapeake historical waterway. (DeAgostini/Getty Images)

The actual mantle worn by Chief Powhatan. Historians are unsure if it was captured during the First Anglo-Powhatan War or if it was gifted during the "coronation" ceremony of Powhatan as an English subject in 1609. (Ashmolean Museum/Heritage Images/Getty Images)

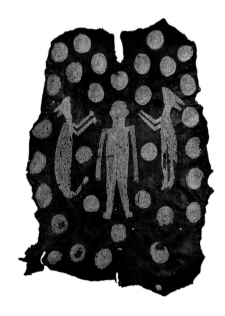

THE POWHATAN CONFEDERACY

Prior to the English arrival, the tribes of the Powhatan, Chickahominy, Pamunkey, and Nansemond rivers had developed a complex sedentary society over the previous 200 years. Anthropologists and historians classify the indigenous people of Virginia as late Woodland peoples of North America. This description helps historians understand how the people of pre-European Virginia lived. Mississippian cultures stretched their influence toward the eastern shores of North America but Woodland groups such as the Powhatans and Monacans retained a distinct way of life. Anthropologically known as Algonquians, Powhatans and their neighbors lived a static lifestyle, building homes for permanent dwelling. Tribes maintained semi-permanent hunting and fishing camps away from their main village. A central plaza surrounded by circular dome dwellings was often constructed. The dwellings consisted of small branches tied in a hatch pattern to create a dome, then bark, skins, and smaller branches rested on top of the hatched dome. This construction kept families warm and dry during the Virginian seasons.

English and Spanish expeditions to the Carolina region in the 1500s provided many sketches and images of what native life looked like. The Powhatan Confederacy lived as static tribes who farmed, built palisaded villages, seasonally fished, and irregularly raided their neighbors for any supply or population shortages in a season. Algonquian culture and religion encouraged trade with one another. Trade demonstrated a tribe's wealth: the more they could trade away, the wealthier it was. Chief Powhatan gained prominence on the Chesapeake through this system of trade and tribute. His six-tribe alliance saw each tribe gifting and trading food and artistic devices such as advanced bead- and shellwork and complex clay pipes. This lifestyle lent itself toward a stable existence and created wealth and large populations.

The archeological record does not portray a significant drop in indigenous population prior to English settlement at Jamestown. This leads many historians to believe the Algonquian and Powhatan peoples encountered Englishmen in a position of strength. Chief Powhatan held sway over as many as 15,000 inhabitants. The historian Helen Rountree reminds readers that Chief Powhatan's confederacy was a subordinate alliance at best, meaning the individuals under his "command" could and often did refuse his wishes. If they paid appropriate tribute and homage, tribes often could pursue their own agendas. The tribes maintained the leeway to trade, negotiate, and even go to war without Chief Powhatan's explicit approval. The confederated tribes lacked citizenship to the confederacy, thereby maintaining their individualistic qualities. The disagreements within a confederation could lead to both Englishmen and Algonquians misunderstanding the broader

This engraving by Theodor de Bry collects nine of John White's watercolors into one image. Painted during the first Roanoke expedition, the images depict the inhabitants of Virginia at European contact. Most notable are the items and dress the Algonquian people carry. (A) Woman with tattoos; (B) Woman with necklace; (C) Priest; (D) Mother with water gourd and child holding English doll; (E) Woman carrying child; (F) Warrior; (G) Weroance; (H) Man in winter wear; (I) Conjurer. (Courtesy of the John Carter Brown Library)

intentions of the other. Often Chief Powhatan himself told English leaders that he desired peace. A subjugated and confederated chief then attacked an English working party and the English leadership criticized Chief Powhatan for lying when his subordinate chief simply raided without approval. As the English population grew, Anglo leadership experienced the same problem with outlying homesteads ignoring mandated guidance from the Jamestown leadership.

Algonquian tribes of the Chesapeake often palisaded their villages. Sleeping structures formed a circle around a central plaza while outside the palisade a large meeting hall enabled visitors to meet without entering the village proper. The writings of the earliest English settlers in Virginia each attempted to tell the history of Chief Powhatan. John Smith and other explorers asked the chieftains how the confederation came about. These writings coupled with archeological findings support a timeline of consolidation for Chief Powhatan prior to the English arrival.

At the turn of the 17th century, Chesapeake Bay teemed with wildlife, navigable rivers, and shallow marshes. This rich land supported Algonquian peoples for generations. Algonquian tribes received little interruption from Europeans before the English landing. Spanish missionaries existed as confusing interlopers to the south but had a negligible effect on their behaviors. Chief Powhatan inherited a six-tribe confederacy from his mother as early as the 1560s and held sway over the tribal towns of Arrohattoc, Appomattoc, Pamunkey, Youghtanund, Mattaponi, and his hometown of Powhatan. This confederacy united primarily to provide food stability between the James (Powhatan), Pamunkey, and Mattaponi rivers as well as to resist Monacan invasions from the west.

In the decades prior to the English landing at Jamestown, Chief Powhatan's ascendency saw continual expansion for his confederacy. First, he incorporated the Paspahegh, Kiskiack, and Werowocomoco tribes who lay downriver from his towns. With the additions of the three tribes, Chief Powhatan controlled modern-day Richmond to Chesapeake Bay.

Examples of Algonquian dwellings at the Chicone Historic Site. (Edwin Remsberg/VW Pics/Universal Images Group via Getty Images)

This image from Robert Beverley's *The History and Present State of Virginia* (1705) depicts the cornfields, rounded dwellings and site for religious ceremonies around poles, and the meeting house is outside the palisade. (Courtesy of the John Carter Brown Library)

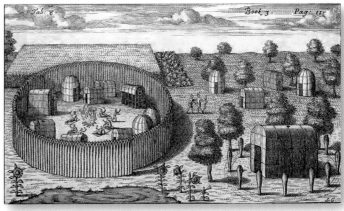

The village of Secoton, North Carolina, drawn in the 1580s by John White. At the bottom of the image is the village's tomb of kings, fire circle, and areas for ceremonial dancing and feasting. Toward the top is its water source, corn crop and gardens. (© The Trustees of the British Museum)

The Chickahominy, located in the center of Chief Powhatan's domain, never submitted to his rule. This tribe remained an ally and partner but according to the Jamestown records they acted independently from Chief Powhatan.

Prior to the turn of the century, Chief Powhatan added the tribes along the Rappahannock and south bank of the Potomac River to his confederacy. Each of the newly added tribes seemed to distance themselves from Powhatan's center of power. The Pissaseck, Moraughtacund, and Rappahannock tribes each moved their capital cities to the north side of the Rappahannock, creating a river's worth of stand-off space between them and the Powhatan Confederacy.

The falls of the James River (modern-day Richmond) created a natural boundary between the Algonquian lands and Siouan peoples to the west. Next, Chief Powhatan incorporated the last downriver tribes. The Nansemond and Kecoughtan tribes submitted to Chief Powhatan, giving him tribute and consulting with him before going to war with neighboring tribes. The 1607 establishment of the Jamestown settlement strained the relationships of the southernmost tribes to Powhatan's power base, between the James and Pamunkey rivers. The last groups brought into Powhatan's confederacy were the extremely resistant tribes on the eastern shore, Accomac and Occohannock. Tribes who resisted saw intense violence and decapitation of their leadership. Chief Powhatan placed loyal sons or nephews in charge of recalcitrant tribes. By 1607 Chief Powhatan controlled the area from the falls of the James River to the islands of the eastern Chesapeake shores.

Networks and Chiefs

The Powhatan Confederacy strengthened the tribes under Chief Powhatan's control through its system of trade and mutual support. This support network became invaluable during severe droughts in the 1580s and 1610s. Tribes within the confederacy easily accessed food stores and allied fighting men. It is arguable that, if the English had not interrupted, the Powhatan Confederacy could have grown into a regional power.

Expanding the confederacy north by joining the tribes of the Potomac River system unleashed a new enemy, the Massawomacks. The Massawomack raiding parties traveled in birch-bark canoes, which were capable of outperforming Powhatan dugout canoes. Northern raiding parties could strike fast into the lower Chesapeake and the dugout canoe-wielding tribes of the Powhatan Confederacy failed to retaliate. This technological weakness played a role in Chief Powhatan's patience with English violence as long as access to technology increased. For defense and food dependability Chief Powhatan's domain seemed to have a stable and growing population prior to 1607.

Growing, trading, and raiding defined the life cycle for the Chesapeake tribes. The fertile lands supplied stable farmlands and many navigable

The Powhatan Confederacy in 1607

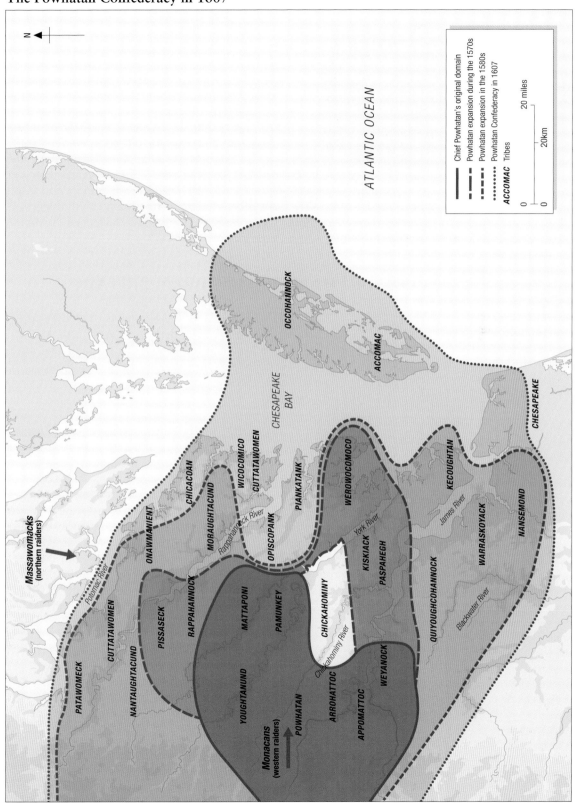

ATLANTIC OCEAN

Chief Powhatan's original domain
Powhatan expansion during the 1570s
Powhatan expansion in the 1580s
Powhatan Confederacy in 1607
ACCOMAC Tribes

0   20 miles
0   20km

N

OCCOHANNOCK

ACCOMAC

CHESAPEAKE BAY

CHESAPEAKE

CHICACOAN

WICOCOMICO

CUTTATAWOMEN

MORAUGHTACUND

PIANKATANK

WEROWOCOMOCO

KECOUGHTAN

ONAWMANIENT

Rappahannock River

OPISCOPANK

York River

KISKIACK

PASPAHEGH

NANSEMOND

Massawomacks
(northern raiders)

Potomac River

CUTTATAWOMEN

PISSASECK

RAPPAHANNOCK

MATTAPONI

PAMUNKEY

CHICKAHOMINY

Chickahominy River

James River

WARRASKOYACK

QUIYOUGHCOHANNOCK

Blackwater River

PATAWOMECK

NANTAUGHTACUND

YOUGHTANUND

POWHATAN

ARROHATTOC

APPOMATTOC

WEYANOCK

Monacans
(western raiders)

9

Powhatan women carried out roles associated with creating. Women were responsible for planting, tending crops, weaving, and raising children. In contrast, men focused on destruction, such as clearing land, hunting, and fighting. (Courtesy of the John Carter Brown Library)

waterways. Towns on the western edge of Powhatan's territory often included a wooden palisade. The Monacan people living at the base of the Appalachians, and the Massawomacks to the north, threatened the tribes of the confederacy with their own seasonal raids to fill gaps in their sustainment systems. Raiding often involved sudden attacks and sabotage.

Spirituality defined martial strength or weakness for Algonquian tribes. In the event of war being declared, chieftains gathered their fighting men and formed a semicircle with a chief or religious leader at the center. The leader of the semicircle would chant, shout, and insult the opposing forces. The leaders believed the man more favored or spiritual would become victorious. The coming of the English challenged Powhatan relationships and spiritual authority.

ELIZABETHAN TO JACOBEAN BRITAIN

The recently united kingdoms of England and Scotland ushered in an era of growth for King James I. Since the 1588 defeat of the Spanish Armada, King James had capitalized on growing British influence through his Danish wife, Queen Anna, and his daughter's marriage to the Spanish Frederick V. King James's foreign policies and increasing debt shaped British decisions throughout the 17th century.

Beginning in 1603, the Jacobean Era benefited from the prior five decades of stability and planning under Elizabeth I. In the previous century, England had barely ranked among the prestigious nations of Europe. Other European peoples utilized strong central governments to mass forces and goods into overseas empires; England jealously looked on.

King James VI of Scotland united England and Scotland upon ascension to the English throne as James I in 1603. (Imagno/Getty Images)

Elizabeth ruled an England which struggled to project itself outside its borders. Decades of dancing along the outskirts of large empires slowly saw English tradesmen find niches within networks to build a way of life and wealth. Trading in the Levant, West Africa, Madagascar, and the Far East, independent English joint-stock companies received money and blessings from the queen to pursue English goals. Through this system of patronage, Elizabeth unlocked an ambitious seaborne merchant class who regularly returned to England with rare, exotic, and expensive merchandise. The English nobility excitedly believed opportunities to raise England's standing coincided with its own rise to wealth.

Henry VIII's legacy lived on in England and helped develop a sense of English Protestants vs Spanish Catholics. The Pope vainly divided the Western Hemisphere between the Spanish and the Portuguese in 1494, driving other nations of Europe to Africa and the Far East. Protestant Elizabeth and her advisers disregarded Papal threats and began seeking room for English growth among the great Spanish domain in America.

The Roanoke colony, placed behind barrier islands, avoided detection from Spanish missions in Florida and the Chesapeake. The colony hoped to remain out of sight, out of mind for Spanish warships. Sir Francis Drake, with a privateer fleet of 27 vessels, prowled Caribbean waters for Spanish

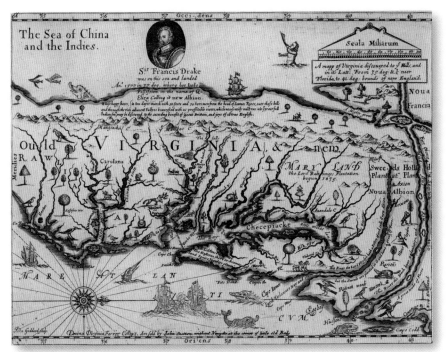

John Farrer's 1651 map gained popularity as a map advocating for English colonization. The map depicts both fantastical and real elements to portray the exotic and daring adventures which awaited future settlers. (Library of Congress, Geography and Map Division)

prizes and promised to resupply the Carolina colony with stolen goods. The first English colonial expedition to the New World saw Ralph Lane, a man who had built his influence through Irish peacekeeping, bring a defensive mindset to the Roanoke colony. Lane's wariness and lack of supply ships led to colonists stealing from the local Manteo tribes, spawning a violent conflict. Lane and his party fled with the next arrival of Drake's fleet.

The second Roanoke attempt by John White and his benefactor Walter Raleigh confidently brought families to the New World, planning to build a lasting home. Virginia Dare, the niece of John White, became the first English birth in the New World. Trade and diplomacy improved with local tribes, but a lack of food caused the local population to mock the English and their inability to sustain themselves.

Desperate for food, John White departed for England, hoping to return with a supply fleet. This small colony hiding on the fringes of Spanish power received a death knell when Spain and England erupted into open conflict. Queen Elizabeth I ordered all English vessels to defend England from the Spanish invasion in 1588, trapping John White in London; he was unable to return to the Carolina coast until 1590, where he found the colony dismantled and abandoned.

Under the rule of Elizabeth, England pursued every opportunity to climb the European ladder. Trade

This 1588 colored engraving by John White and Theodor de Bry shows the landward view to approach the Roanoke colony. The artistic map shows a protected harbor but with many mystical creatures and threats in the area. (DeAgostini/Getty Images)

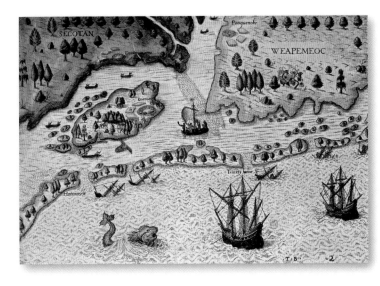

Drake's activity in the Atlantic exemplifies the English desire to compete with Spain at any cost. (Buyenlarge/Getty Images)

stations in Syria, failed colonies in Madagascar and America, successful settlements in Ireland, and paid privateer vessels prowled the Caribbean and Indian Ocean. Queen Elizabeth empowered the joint-stock company known as the East India Trading Company with rights and powers to trade in the Indian Ocean. From 1601 onward, the sudden success of the East India Trading Company inspired more joint ventures.

FOUNDING JAMESTOWN

By 1605, James I desired a permanent foothold to challenge Spanish power and seek English wealth. A team of 104 adventurers departed England on December 19, 1606 and the three vessels arrived at Cape Henry, Virginia, on April 26, 1607. After 128 days at sea, the Englishmen scouted for a suitable location to land permanently. The crews toured far up the newly named James River. They watched as Native Americans appeared along the riverbanks to gawk at the three unknown vessels tacking back and forth. The three ship captains, Christopher Newport, Bartholomew Gosnold, and John Ratcliffe, turned the ships downstream and agreed upon a landing site which appeared to be a secluded island separated from local villages by several miles. They landed the *Susan Constant*, *Godspeed*, and *Discovery* along the banks of the island. The land there steeply fell into the Chesapeake, enabling the crews to throw ropes ashore and pull the vessels right up to the shoreline. All three ships soon moored to sturdy Virginia trees as the 104 adventurers debarked and began searching for ways to capitalize on their stay in Virginia.

John Smith, a veteran of wars in Turkey, Holland, and Ireland, brought his worldly knowledge to the table to ensure the Jamestown colony survived. A council of gentlemen bickered and failed to agree how to run the new settlement. The adventurers who arrived did not intend to be colonists; they hoped to find quick wealth through conquest, trade with the local peoples, or mining then return to England. Since the days of Queen Elizabeth, English adventurers often acted aggressively and ignored consequences, planning on a rapid departure. The Virginia Company hoped to make the settlement permanent but as more of a trade station than as a town.

The first president elected for the Jamestown council warned the adventurers that if they built a palisade wall the local tribes would assume they came to fight and could become hostile. This warning caused the settlers to construct only crude dwellings during their first weeks in Virginia. This ended abruptly on May 26, 1607, when 200 Paspahegh warriors surrounded and harried the English beachhead. The Englishmen had yet to unpack their weapons from the shipping crates, causing the attack to be resisted only by cannon fire from the *Discovery* and *Godspeed*. The cannonade scattered the attacking warriors. The attack wounded 11 men and killed one young cabin boy, Robert Mutton. Within 27 days of landing in Virginia the first Englishman had died from an attack by the local people. Feelings of fear and a renewed drive for survival overwhelmed the settlers. Leaders now sought ways to build an alliance with the local people, knowing that at any moment the neighboring tribes had the ability to drive the small beachhead settlement into the river.

The rest of 1607 saw the gentlemen disagreeing over how to proceed, but small parties began venturing farther from Jamestown in search of trade or minerals. By December 1607, only half of the party survived; some had died from disease or had disappeared while foraging and exploring. One man of action, John Smith, avoided the strife and death by taking a small crew to explore the surrounding region. Smith and two others explored the Chickahominy River in search of food. At the Powhatan village of Orapax, the exploration ended with his companions killed and Smith taken prisoner.

By the end of December 1607, only 37 Englishmen survived, and John Smith was assumed dead. Miraculously, Smith endured his capture; during which Chief Opechancanough paraded him to several key villages. From these travels Smith learned of the complex confederacy maintained by Chief Powhatan and developed a relationship with both Opechancanough and Powhatan; he promised the chief that, if released, he would make peace between their peoples. Chief Powhatan accepted Smith as a subordinate confederated chief, or weroance; he released Smith on the condition that Smith uphold his role as a lesser weroance. Smith departed and reappeared in Jamestown in January, only days before the arrival of the first resupply.

Jamestown's 400th anniversary saw the recreation of the three English ships arriving in Virginia. (Adrin Snider/Newport News Daily Press/Tribune News Service via Getty Images)

SUPPLYING THE COLONY

The Virginia Company learned from the mistakes of previous settlement attempts and planned for resupply ships to continually return to Jamestown. Captain Newport arrived for the second time to Jamestown in January 1608. With Newport's support, John Smith was elected president of the settlement. Smith provided direction and a strict regime for farming and construction. He developed a system where all men of the colony proved their worth. The 38 original surviving adventurers were supplemented with a new contingent of 73 men. No women arrived until the second supply. The disappointed company leaders back in England sent more laborers and tradesmen, hoping to spur on the economy. Yet, in the new batch of settlers 28 men claimed gentlemen status. These gentlemen challenged Smith's leadership as they did not expect to be tasked by a military man. Smith advocated for draconian rules and encouraged the men of Jamestown to plant, hoping to cultivate a sustainable future for the colony. The class of gentlemen did not see themselves as planters or colonists but adventurers.

Relying on his relationship with Chief Powhatan, John Smith sought alliances with the nearby tribes. Chief Powhatan specifically prevented the Monacan and Delaware tribes from interacting with the English presence, thereby ensuring the newcomers depended on his support for survival.

Attempting to expand English knowledge and avoid entrapment by Chief Powhatan, Smith departed with a team to explore the Chesapeake by boat.

Attack on initial Jamestown encampment, May 1607 (PP. 14–15)

After establishing a beachhead and small encampment on what would become the Jamestown Peninsula, Captain Newport and other leaders of the Virginia Company sailed north to explore upriver, leaving the *Godspeed* and *Discovery* moored at the shoreline (**1**).

English adventurers continued to establish the campsite. No fortifications had been constructed and no permanent structures completed (**2**) when, suddenly, 200 Paspahegh Warriors emerged from the tree line and began unleashing arrows toward the Englishmen (**3**). The Englishmen struggled to reach weapons as most firearms remained packed inside "dry fats," or wooden shipment chests (**4**). As the attack unfolded, a few men on board the moored vessels loaded the small deck cannons of the two ships and opened fire on the warriors (**5**). The cannon fire launched several shots into the formation, but when a cannonball struck a tree, dropping it in front of the warriors, the massed formation withdrew (**6**).

Smith recorded dozens of local villages along the rivers and inlets of the Chesapeake and created a highly detailed map (see page 4) which portrayed a fertile land of rolling hills and forests filled with the Powhatan, Monacan, and other Algonquian tribes. Smith lists animals and rivers ripe for exploitation. On the map, two large characters appear. On the top left, Chief Powhatan sits in council over his subordinate chiefs as witnessed by Smith during his captivity. And

on the right edge a large depiction of a Susquehannock chief is portrayed. In Smith's writings he describes the depicted chieftain as a large and powerful warrior and as a beautiful specimen of a man. This description highlights the martial mentality with which Smith viewed his opponents. He sized up each chief or warrior, and determined if he could beat him in a fight.

This original woodcut depicts John Smith fighting back against his captors, but then being hampered by marshy terrain. (mikroman6/ Getty Images)

The explorations and mapping done by John Smith portray an incredibly complex Chesapeake world. The map has dozens of villages. The many labels portray the densely populated networks concentrated on waterways. Game and resources appear on the map in appropriate places. Smith even indicated with small black Maltese crosses the farthest extent of his personal observations. He describes that all details beyond the indicated crosses were determined from trade and retelling by the local population. The map created by John Smith during his two exploratory journeys captures the Powhatan world better than any other document in existence.

After Smith's captivity, he routinely visited Chief Powhatan and Chief Opechancanough. Under Powhatan customs two types of chiefs ruled the tribes, war chiefs and peace chiefs. Opechancanough acted as Powhatan's primary war chief. Many historians see Smith's respect toward Opechancanough as his efforts to reassure the Powhatan war chief of his peaceful intentions. Smith grasped the fledgling English settlement's position of weakness.

The second supply arrived in September 1608, bringing 67 new settlers to Jamestown. This group added 26 more gentlemen seeking quick riches and glory. The first two women arrived, a wife and her maid. Eight of the laborers were described as "glassmen." They created the first glasshouse in the colony and helped search for a usable product to produce in Virginia. Before

Designed for the 400th anniversary in 2007, this sloop is an exact recreation of the sloop used by John Smith during his exploration of the Chesapeake. (Mark Gail/*The Washington Post* via Getty Images)

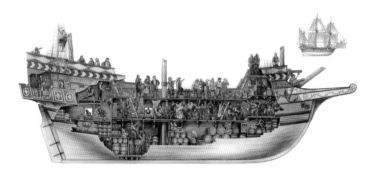

The *Susan Constant* was the largest of the three ships. The first landing in 1607 carried minimal supplies, intending to plant and trade for sustainment. This cross section depicts how life could have looked on the ship packed tightly with the Virginia Company adventurers. (Tribune News Service via Getty Images)

departing once again for England, Captain Newport presented Chief Powhatan with a crown and robe to symbolize their alliance. Two mutual misunderstandings existed between the Powhatans and the English. Chief Powhatan believed that John Smith's submission as a weroance established the settlement as a confederated town. The Jamestown council believed Chief Powhatan's acceptance of the robe and crown demonstrated his understanding as a subordinate ruler to the English king. For a time, this misunderstanding created peace because both sides assumed the other sought to please them.

This brief period of peace ruptured in January 1609 when John Smith visited Chief Powhatan at the capital of Werowocomoco. Smith refused to disarm in the chief's presence. This signaled to Chief Powhatan that Smith was a weroance in rebellion to Powhatan, and small this-for-that raids began progressively escalating between Powhatans and Englishmen.

In August 1609, Captain Newport and the third supply intended to arrive with seven ships, 300 passengers, and new leadership for the colony. The fleet separated in a great storm, preventing the flagship *Sea Venture* from reaching Jamestown until later. The remaining ships which did arrive brought an influx of people who spurred the colony toward rapid expansion. The new settlers comprised families who constructed homesteads increasingly farther away from the now robust five-sided fort at Jamestown, expanding the English presence. With the delay of the *Sea Venture*, John Smith gained a few more weeks as the leader of the colony. The growing raids and counter-raids became worse between the two sides but Smith's continual communication with Chief Powhatan prevented all-out war.

After a mysterious explosion injured John Smith, Captain Samuel Argall, a ship's master who arrived in the third supply, took Smith and the supply ships back to England. With the departure of Smith, leadership of the colony fell to George Percy. Smith's departure not only emboldened many of the gentlemen to resist farming but also signaled to Powhatan leaders that no Englishman with a true relationship to the confederacy remained in the colony. With Smith's departure the Powhatans simultaneously attacked outlying English settlements and Chief Powhatan began a multi-month siege of Jamestown Island. This common Algonquian tactic was intended to bring recalcitrant tribes back into obedience. The settlers congregated into Jamestown Fort and triggered the "starving time." The first war between the English and the tribes of the Powhatan Confederacy had begun.

Powhatans desired the technology brought by the English. Trade became standard between the settlers and the tribes. Artwork by Sydney King for the National Park Service. (MPI/Getty Images)

Events of 1607–10

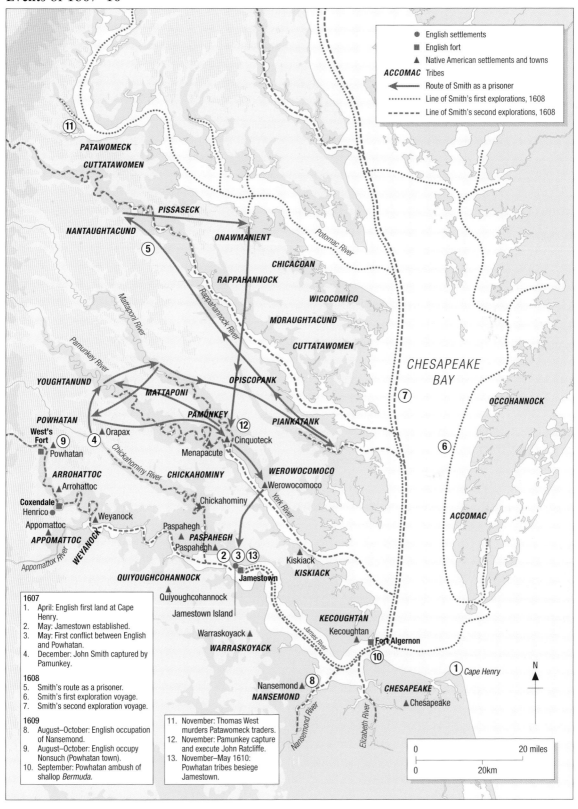

Legend:
- ● English settlements
- ■ English fort
- ▲ Native American settlements and towns
- *ACCOMAC* Tribes
- ← Route of Smith as a prisoner
- ⋯ Line of Smith's first explorations, 1608
- - - Line of Smith's second explorations, 1608

CHESAPEAKE BAY

PATAWOMECK
CUTTATAWOMEN
⑪
PISSASECK
NANTAUGHTACUND
ONAWMANIENT
⑤
CHICACOAN
RAPPAHANNOCK
WICOMICO
MORAUGHTACUND
CUTTATAWOMEN
OCCOHANNOCK
YOUGHTANUND
OPISCOPANK
⑦
MATTAPONI
PAMUNKEY
PIANKATANK
POWHATAN
West's Fort ⑨ ④ ▲ Orapax
⑫ ▲ Cinquoteck
⑥
Menapacute
ACCOMAC
■ Powhatan
ARROHATTOC
▲ Arrohattoc
CHICKAHOMINY
WEROWOCOMOCO
▲ Werowocomoco
Coxendale
Henrico ●
Chickahominy
Appomattoc
▲ Weyanock
APPOMATTOC
Paspahegh
WEYANOCK
▲ PASPAHEGH
Paspahegh ▲
② ③ ⑬
QUIYOUGHCOHANNOCK
Kiskiack
▲
Jamestown
KISKIACK
Quiyoughcohannock
Jamestown Island
KECOUGHTAN
Warraskoyack ▲
Kecoughtan
WARRASKOYACK
Fort Algernon ■
⑩
① Cape Henry
Nansemond ▲ ⑧
CHESAPEAKE
NANSEMOND
▲ Chesapeake

Rivers: Potomac River, Rappahannock River, Mattaponi River, Pamunkey River, Chickahominy River, York River, James River, Appomattox River, Nansemond River, Elizabeth River

N

1607
1. April: English first land at Cape Henry.
2. May: Jamestown established.
3. May: First conflict between English and Powhatan.
4. December: John Smith captured by Pamunkey.

1608
5. Smith's route as a prisoner.
6. Smith's first exploration voyage.
7. Smith's second exploration voyage.

1609
8. August–October: English occupation of Nansemond.
9. August–October: English occupy Nonsuch (Powhatan town).
10. September: Powhatan ambush of shallop *Bermuda*.

11. November: Thomas West murders Patawomeck traders.
12. November: Pamunkey capture and execute John Ratcliffe.
13. November–May 1610: Powhatan tribes besiege Jamestown.

0 _____ 20 miles
0 _____ 20km

CHRONOLOGY

1607

May — Three vessels arrive on the James River. They agree to land and establish the settlement of Jamestown on a small island surrounded by marshlands, distant from the nearest villages.

May 26 — First attack on the Jamestown settlement by 200 warriors. Shipboard cannon fire disperses the attack.

December — John Smith departs the sickly settlement to explore and build alliances. Powhatan warriors capture Smith and keep him in captivity for four weeks. During this time, Smith meets several Powhatan chieftains and learns the terrain.

1608

January — The first supply arrives, saving the struggling and sick settlers. John Smith appears miraculously from captivity as an allied weroance of Chief Powhatan.

Summer — John Smith explores each tributary of Chesapeake Bay.

September — The fort of Jamestown expands into a five-sided palisade with ramparts.

December — The second supply arrives with more gentlemen, laborers, and the settlement's first two women.

1609

January — Stressed about obtaining food, Smith meets with Chief Powhatan and others, aggressively pushing for trade. These violent encounters label Smith as a weroance in rebellion against Powhatan, and relations sour.

August — The remnants of the third supply arrive with more than 300 settlers, including women and children.

September — Chief Powhatan relocates his capital village from Powhatan town to Orapax town, farther from English reach and away from water access.

October — The third supply departs for England, taking a wounded John Smith away from the colony.

November — The English–Powhatan alliance lacks personal relationships, and Chief Powhatan orders the siege of Jamestown.

1610

May — Chief Powhatan lifts the siege of Jamestown. Of the 410 Englishmen in the settlement before the siege, 60 survived the besieged "starving time."

June — Thomas Gates, acting leader of the settlement, attempts to abandon the colony but encounters the fourth supply led by Baron De La Warr, who orders a return to Jamestown.

July — Start of First Anglo-Powhatan War: De La Warr empowers Thomas Gates to go on the offensive against the Powhatan tribes. Gates leads an armored English company to raid and destroy the village of Kecoughtan – the first English offensive in the New World.

August — George Percy leads a second English offensive, attacking the village of Paspahegh.

1611

May — Thomas Dale arrives at Jamestown with 300 veteran soldiers.

June — Thomas Dale leads an English offensive to destroy several towns of the Nansemond tribe.

August   Thomas Gates returns to Jamestown, bringing more veteran soldiers, whom De La Warr takes to establish a new fortified settlement, Henrico, at the falls of the James River.

1613

April   Captain Samuel Argall captures Chief Powhatan's favored daughter, Pocahontas.

1614

March   Thomas Dale and a large force threaten destruction of the Pamunkey town of Matchot. The stand-off of forces leads to a meeting between Pocahontas and her brothers, promising peace to the English.

April   Chief Powhatan negotiates with the Jamestown leaders, culminating with the marriage of Pocahontas to John Rolfe, restoring the relational alliance.

1618

Spring   Death of Chief Powhatan. Years of relative peace followed the marriage of 1614. The leadership of the confederacy fell to Powhatan's brother Opitchapam, becoming Chief Itoyatin.

November   Arrival of the Great Charter removes martial law for the first time in Jamestown. Establishment of the head-right system and a general assembly called the House of Burgesses.

1620

April   A census of the colony finds 1,235 people living within the settlements of the Jamestown colony: 898 men, 141 women, 192 children, and four 'Indians.'

1622

March 22   Years of relative peace are shattered by hundreds of Powhatan warriors coordinating an attack which kills over 347 colonists and begins the Second Anglo-Powhatan War.

Winter   Devastation from the spring attacks sees hundreds perish from starvation and disease in cramped besieged fortresses.

1623

May   The English host a faux negotiation council where 200 chiefs, including Opechancanough, are poisoned. Opechancanough survives but ill health prevents him from leading war parties for several years.

1624

June   Governor Francis Wyatt leads an armored musketeer company against the Pamunkey villages, in the largest battle of the war.

1625

March   Charles I is crowned King of Britain. He revokes the Virginia Company charter redesignating it as a Royal Colony.

1625–31

Seasonal raids and counter-raids continue a cycle of violence.

1632

The English and Powhatans agree to a peace treaty led by Opechancanough and Governor John Harvey bringing about the end of the Second Anglo-Powhatan War.

1634

Construction of the Great Palisade is completed, walling off the Virginia Peninsula from Powhatan raiding.

1644

April   Chief Opechancanough executes one last coordinated attack on the Virginia colony killing 490 colonists.

OPPOSING COMMANDERS

In the 17th century only rare leaders could personally impact the battlefields of Europe. Yet conflicts in 17th-century Virginia relied heavily on the expertise and guidance of war captains and leaders. Small-scale raids and open field battles needed experienced leaders to overcome opponents. Alongside the clash of Old World and New World cultures, technologies of the late renaissance evolved into early modern warfare with disorienting effects. The 80 Years' War surrounded the period of early English settlement with significant impact on the leadership and tactics used in the New World. This section develops a short biography on each of the key leaders of the first and second Anglo-Powhatan wars.

English captains' and commanders' individual skills greatly effected the smaller engagements of Virginia. For example, John Smith and Thomas Dale personally grappled with enemy combatants during conflict and negotiations. On the Powhatan side, they experienced technology in flux as indigenous nations to the north, west, and south challenged Powhatan lands with burgeoning European trade goods. The war and peace chiefs of the confederacy carried immense influence into each exchange with the English adventurers.

Both the Jamestown colony and the Powhatan Confederacy experienced revolving leaders whose often conflicting visions muddied campaign plans. The first Anglo-Powhatan conflict from 1609 to 1614 and the second conflict from 1622 to 1632 both rose and fell based on the relationship of internal leaders and their reactions to the opposite faction.

War chiefs and famous warriors played key roles in Powhatan negotiations and martial events. Cloaks, paint, war clubs, and war feathers marked illustrious Powhatan leaders. This art piece by Peter Dennis depicts Chief Powhatan sitting with war chiefs and a shaman reacting to prisoners nearby. (Peter Dennis/Getty Images)

The Powhatan Confederacy followed a chief-of-chiefs, held by Wahunsenacawh (known to the English and his subordinate chiefs as Chief Powhatan), and a war-chief-of-war-chiefs, held by Opechancanough. Powhatan people titled the chief-of-chiefs the Mamanatowick. As such the leaders assumed a new chiefly name. Wahunsenacawh became known publicly as Chief Powhatan upon his assumption of the leadership role. These two men held the confederacy together and balanced the wants and needs of many subordinate chieftains. Chieftains of villages far from Chief Powhatan's reach often acted unexpectedly, challenging his authority. Powhatan leadership did not have centralized control but a unified vision stemming from Chief Powhatan.

The early leaders of Jamestown brought diverse backgrounds in English governance, and many brought experience from Irish, Turkish, or Catholic conflicts. Christopher Newport, John Smith, Thomas West, George Yeardley, and other English leaders often acted independently pursuing their own vision for the colony. Conflicting visions often hampered negotiations of another or led to violence in one region and peace in another. Chief Powhatan faced a similar dilemma as each of his subordinate chieftains of the confederacy acted independently for trade and often raiding. English adventurers and gentlemen expected eventual departure from the colony which caused many leaders to act aggressively and quickly to leave a mark on the colony and vacate before consequences took effect. Individual English gentlemen often sought their own wealth and safety over the success of the nascent colony.

Recurring supplies and fresh men kept the colony alive. Artwork by Sydney King for the National Park Service. (MPI/Getty Images)

English and Powhatan leaders defined the conflicts. Sometimes as a unified group, often as disunified regional warlords. Chief Powhatan held sway over dozens of outlying tribes and villages who often tested his authority. Each English leader of Jamestown likewise expanded the English zone and held authority over multiplying homesteads and plantations, often flouting Jamestown's authority.

Clothing in warmer weather was sparse but Powhatans often covered all exposed skin in red paint from Poconos root. This watercolor was painted by John White in the 1580s. (© The Trustees of the British Museum)

POWHATAN LEADERS, THE MAMANATOWICK

Three key leaders led the Powhatan peoples through the Anglo-Powhatan wars. Chief Powhatan held the title of Mamanatowick, or chief-of-chiefs, from 1586 to 1618. Chief Itoyatin succeeded Chief Powhatan from 1618 to 1629. Chief Opechancanough served as war-chief-of-war-chiefs under both of his elder brothers and ascended to the paramount chief position in 1629 until his death in 1646.

Chief Powhatan, Wahunsenacawh

He is of personage a tall well proportioned man, with a sower looke, his head somwhat gray, his beard so thinne, that it seemeth none at all, his age neare sixtie; of a very able and hardy body to endure any labour. About his person ordinarily attendeth a guard of 40 or 50 of the tallest men his Countrey doth afford. Every night and watch upon the foure quarters of his house are foure Sentinels, each from other a flight shoot [arrow's shot], and at every halfe houre one from the Corps du guard doth hollow, shaking his lips with his finger betweene them; unto whom every Sentinell doth answer round from his stand [whistle callout to each guard]: if any faile, they presently send forth an officer that beateth him extremely.

So writes John Smith in his 1624 cumulative work on his knowledge of Virginia, *A Generall Historie of Virginia and the Summer Isles*. Powhatan's size, influence, and ingenuity established him as the premier leader of the Powhatan Confederacy. John Smith's description of Chief Powhatan portrays a powerful ruler capable of ruling his domain. The Chief-of-Chiefs, King, Emperor, Despot, have all described Wahunsenacawh. Wahunsenacawh came to power as a young warrior. Receiving his right to leadership through his mother, possibly a princess of the Patawomeck tribe who married into the Powhatan tribe. Upon the death of his father (also named Wahunsenacawh), Wahunsenacawh remained the highest-ranking son and assumed dominance over the six-tribe alliance as early as 1580. As the ranking chief of the Confederacy, he acted as a peace chief. This role fit Wahunsenacawh well as he masterly negotiated and subdued many tribes without direct warfare. Wahunsenacawh led the Powhatan Confederacy as Chief Powhatan until 1618. During that time, he extended influence through traditional Algonquian ways. Methods such as a gift giving, intermarriage, ambassadors using wampum and pipes, siege, kidnapping of leaders, assassination of leaders, or burning storehouses all expanded Chief Powhatan's realm.

In 1580, the Powhatan Confederacy lay between the James and Mattaponi rivers. This small yet fertile area enabled the confederated tribes to live a static agrarian life; as such, they often stored food surpluses, eating well even in seasons of drought or war. English writers repeatedly described Chief Powhatan and his fellow Powhatan warriors as robust and large men. The secure and well-fed lifestyle of Chief Powhatan clashes with stereotypical views many historians hold of Native Americans. Even a well-renowned scholar of the first people of Virginia disagrees with John Smith, saying that he was exaggerating to make Chief Powhatan sound fiercer. A disregard for Smith's physical descriptions of Powhatan chiefs conflicts with the evidence of Smith's life story. Smith rose to fame after victoriously dueling his former enslaver and demonstrating combat skill for several years as a mercenary in Holland and the Ottoman lands. Yet he claims Powhatan warriors overcame him twice to capture and subdue him. When he writes that a Powhatan warrior was larger than him, his description speaks from experience of physical defeat. Perhaps the Powhatan warriors may have lacked the height Smith described, but they still possessed greater strength of arms to subdue Smith. Historians who call the Powhatan warriors small cross-country runners are confusing the static agrarian life of the 17th-century Algonquians with the nomadic life of other people groups.

Powhatan's size, influence, and ingenuity established him as the premier leader of the Powhatan Confederacy and a worthy adversary to the nascent

Returning from captivity, John Smith explained an impressive scene entering the "emporerers" presence. The great chief Powhatan had women on either side of him and many men and women in attendance below his platform. This German edition of Smith's 1612 woodcut captures the grandeur of the meeting house and Powhatan town. (Courtesy of the John Carter Brown Library)

English colony. From the first appearance of English sailors at Cape Henry and their subsequent testing of the upper James River, Chief Powhatan commanded his subjugated chiefs to inform, observe, and interact with the newcomers. Chief Powhatan treated the newly arrived Englishmen as the wayward tribe they were. He rapidly evaluated them and correctly assessed that their lack of women and families indicated either short-term stay or a warlike people. The 1607 capture of John Smith provided the exact opportunity Chief Powhatan had hoped for to bring the Englishmen under his domain.

John Smith, as a captive, paraded from village to village and saw the strength, wealth, and interconnected network of the Powhatan people. After this tour Chief Powhatan staged a dramatic event where he pretended to kill Smith and a tribal princess intervened on his behalf. This showmanship indebted Smith to the chief and conveyed the possibility of future intermarriage to a tribal chief who could submit and obey. John Smith departed captivity in January of 1608 as a subjugated weroance to Chief Powhatan. Weroance means commander, specifically a leader below the Mamanatowick. From then on Chief Powhatan expected John Smith and his English tribe to behave as any other subjugated weroance. Chief Powhatan expected each weroance to follow his general vision although they could sometimes disregard his authority in local matters, often leading to trade disputes or even violence between tribes. The Mamanatowick can be thought of as a captain-of-captains or a chief-of-chiefs, but the Powhatans did not hold to a divine right of rule; all weroances obeyed as a sign of respect and honor. Whoever held the highest rank, determined first by matrilineal spiritual authority, followed by the father's political rank, had the duty to lead. For example, while Chief Powhatan lived, his successors Opitchapam and Opechancanough loyally followed him. Upon Powhatan's death Opechancanough respected Opitchapam's ascension even though it caused problems for the confederacy.

Powhatan towns had rectangular-shaped bark- and skin-covered homes and nearby family farms with large cornfields a short walk away. (Peter Dennis/Getty Images)

Itoyatin struggled to connect and lead as well as Powhatan and Opechancanough. Under Chief Itoyatin's leadership several of the more independent tribes left the confederacy.

For John Smith and his newly established relationship beneath Chief Powhatan, if Smith responded and obeyed when Chief Powhatan called, Chief Powhatan contentedly allowed the Englishmen to expand and trade with the Powhatan network. Chief Powhatan's leadership perspective hoped to capitalize on the arrival of a new tribe who possessed unknown technologies and offered men capable of joining in a war party. When John Smith departed in October 1609, the English stopped responding to Chief Powhatan's demands, therefore Chief Powhatan responded in the same way he would respond to any other subjugated tribe who began disobeying, by laying siege until they capitulated.

Viewing Chief Powhatan's actions through a lens of how he expected subordinate tribes

This 1706 woodcut interprets two scenes. On the left Smith observes a religious ceremony. The right is the notorious scene of Pocahontas' saving of Smith which more likely was part of a larger religious ceremony incorporating Smith as a weroance. (Courtesy of the John Carter Brown Library)

to behave helps to humanize and make sense of actions that from a European perspective can seem like a sudden change of emotions. Chief Powhatan hoped to incorporate into his confederacy the technology of the advanced yet seemingly small English tribe who appeared on his shores.

Chief Itoyatin, Opitchapam

Algonquian lineage relied on a mother's line to establish rank, then the father's position to determine eligibility for leadership. Opitchapam ranked second among Chief Powhatan's weroances (chiefs), as Chief Powhatan's half-brother from the same mother. Opitchapam ruled the Pamunkey tribe controlling several towns along the Pamunkey River. John Smith first met Opitchapam as a captive at the Pamunkey town of Menapacute. Opitchapam's close relationship with the chief-of-chiefs put him in many of the first encounters with the English adventurers. Upon establishment of the Jamestown settlement, Opitchapam served as a chief diplomat for Chief Powhatan, opening negotiations and trade with the newly arrived men.

From the writings of John Smith, Opitchapam often traveled with his young brother Kekataugh. Kekataugh may have been a half-brother through his father as he did not fall into the Powhatan line of succession. Together they often met with John Smith for trade and negotiations. Interestingly, all three half-brothers of Chief Powhatan met at the town of Cinquoteck during John Smith's captivity. The three chiefs, Opechancanough, Opitchapam, and Kekataugh, staged a mock battle where they created two companies of 100 men to demonstrate the Powhatan way of war.

The leadership of the three chiefs rapidly planned and executed the mock battle demonstrating high communication, understanding, and trust between the three men who each ruled large tribes and sections within the Powhatan Confederacy. The mock battle witnessed by Smith in late 1608 may have been an exercise involving Pamunkey, Youghtanund, and Mattaponi tribesmen. Creating joint training events on short notice indicates the three tribes' familiarity and respect, working together to understand easily and quickly the intentions of Opechancanough, the war chief of the Powhatans.

A second key event led by Opitchapam occurred during the tense negotiations in the fall of 1609. John Smith quarreled with Opitchapam and Powhatan, threatening and bartering for more trade goods from the town of Potaunacack. Opitchapam's son attempted to poison the trading party over dinner. Smith wrote that the poison failed to kill the Englishmen who consumed it, but it did make them all sick until they expelled it. Despite Opitchapam's willingness to threaten John Smith and the other English, he played a critical role in ending the first Anglo-Powhatan conflict. In 1614, after five years of raids and counter-raids, Opitchapam acted as Pocahontas' escort to her marriage with John Rolfe. The writings of Percy, Smith, and

Strachey all describe Opitchapam as the "old uncle" who gave Pocahontas away.

Chief Itoyatin ascended to the leadership of the Powhatan Confederacy upon Chief Powhatan's death in 1618. Samuel Purchas described Opitchapam, now known as Chief Itoyatin, as "decrepit and old." Although Opitchapam's rank enabled him to lead the confederacy, Opechancanough began to take control of the tribes. Opitchapam led as a figurehead. His role as the peace chief diminished as the war chief Opechancanough pursued plans to eliminate the English.

This 1885 painting by Henry Brueckner depicts Pocahontas' marriage with many inaccuracies, but one important truth is that Chief Opitchapam and another Powhatan man are present at the ceremony. (Kean Collection/Getty Images)

The Second Anglo-Powhatan War saw Opitchapam primarily coordinate logistics for the confederacy as Opechancanough, the war chief, coordinated the attacks on the Jamestown settlements. By the conflict's conclusion, Opechancanough was injured and sick. Opitchapam personally led the last major encounter of the conflict in 1624. Despite boasting of his warriors' strength, Opitchapam did not have the warrior skills of Opechancanough; even with 800 Pamunkey bowmen he failed to stop the English force from burning his fields of corn. After Opitchapam's defeat in 1624, the Pamunkey remained on the defensive for the rest of the war. His death in 1629 finally promoted Opechancanough to the position of Mamanatowick, chief-of-chiefs. The lineage of Chief Powhatan continued.

Chief Mangopeesomon, Opechancanough, and Paquiquineo

Powhatan and other Virginian Native American leaders have very little known about them. The scarcity of preserved written information from this era forces historians to rely heavily on the works of John Smith, George Percy, and other English writers of the time. Most facts about Chief Powhatan, Itoyatin, or the Monacans come from these sources. According to English writers, Opechancanough was the third half-brother of Chief Powhatan and led the Powhatan tribe as its war chief for many years. He died at the age of 102, if John Smith correctly cited his age.

Historians debate additional sources related to Opechancanough. An alternate name some historians believe applied to Opechancanough is Paquiquineo. If Paquiquineo and Opechancanough are the same man, a fascinating portion of early Chesapeake history can be united.

As a young boy, Paquiquineo found himself face to face with Spanish explorers in 1561. Those explorers enticed the young man on to their ship and took him to Spain to present to King Philip II. Paquiquineo received an allowance and clothing stipend from the king befitting him his claimed rank as the son of a great king of Bahía de Santa Maria (Chesapeake). While in Spain, Paquiquineo learned Spanish, the Christian religion, and changed his name to Don Luís. After seven years in Spain, Don Luís discovered that a Jesuit mission, the Ajácan, had recently begun near the Pamunkey and Chickahominy rivers, very near the location of his capture. He offered to return to America as a

Catholic missionary to his own people. Don Luís encouraged other Spaniards to join him, boasting of the fertility of the Chesapeake region. The Jesuits agreed and formed a resupply party to travel to Bahía de Santa Maria. Don Luís professed the goal of finding his original tribe to bring them the Christian religion. Paquiquineo arrived at the Spanish Mission in 1570. Nine years after his capture, Don Luís returned to his homeland, having learned much about the Spanish, European, and Christian way of life.

For a year, the Spanish Mission on the edge of Chesapeake Bay struggled to take hold, receiving no further Spanish aid or supplies. The Jesuit missionaries relied on Don Luís as their translator and negotiator. Primary sources tell us Father Segura, the head of the Jesuit mission, and the other missionaries feared Don Luís, knowing they relied fully on his friendship and protection for survival. After a year of struggling, the winter of 1570/71 led to starvation and weakness for the transplanted Jesuits. Don Luís took this opportunity to turn the tables on his new European relationships and, accompanied by several native warriors and wearing European clothes, entered Father Segura's home in a friendly manner. Once the number of Jesuits and natives reached equality, the warriors struck out and killed each Jesuit simultaneously. Historian James Horn evaluates Paquiquineo's "betrayal" as a logical step, arguing that it "reestablished him among his people and symbolized his utter rejection of Spanish ways and his European life. Don Luís was no more; he was once again Paquiquineo." Paquiquineo's return marked the start of the first cycle of surprise ambushes upon European interlopers.

Helen Rountree, author of numerous works on 17th-century Virginia, firmly believes that Paquiquineo and Opechancanough were two different men. Rountree explains that the matrilineal succession of the Powhatan people prevents Opechancanough from becoming Paquiquineo. She believes Paquiquineo lived farther south than the Powhatan region and had no connection to the Jamestown settlement, citing the lack of Spanish references written in English records and absence of Spanish goods in Powhatan towns. In contrast, James Horn, the current president of Jamestown Rediscovery, argues Opechancanough was the same person as Paquiquineo, dismissing Rountree's concerns, pointing to what is known of the end of the Spanish Mission in the Chesapeake. A lone survivor of the Ajácan attack reported that Paquiquineo and his men attempted to erase all remains of the Spanish Mission, hoping to prevent future ships from discovering the location again. In *A Brave and Cunning Prince*, Horn spends the first half of the book arguing that Paquiquineo's early life experiences line up with the future actions taken by Opechancanough. If Opechancanough was Paquiquineo, this carries major significance for military history and the study of the decision-making processes pursued by Chief Opechancanough.

Spanish settlements often began as a mission. Jesuit priests boldly attempted missionary work in hostile lands. (Interim Archives/ Getty Images)

The surprise attack of 1571 incorporates many similarities to the attack of 1622, which will be discussed in depth later in this work. If Opechancanough really did spend nearly a decade among Europeans, he would have understood what European settlement and religious conversion meant. He would have spoken many languages, Powhatan-Algonquian, Spanish, and English. All things that could have altered his motives and actions. He would have utilized his knowledge of Spanish expansion and religion to lull his enemies into a well-timed destruction. Opechancanough pursued Christianity and entangled trading partnerships with the Jamestown plantations until he gave a signal to kill all Englishmen. Opechancanough nearly drove English colonization back into the sea in 1622.

The evolving names for Opechancanough end with a final change to Mangopeesomon in 1620. Helen Rountree believes Opechancanough's final name change represented his preparations for the great assault of 1622. Rising to the Mamanatowick role by 1629, Opechancanough executed a final cycle of feigned friendship followed by murder in 1644. This Third Anglo-Powhatan War ended quickly with Opechancanough's capture. Robert Beverley wrote in his 1705 *History of Virginia*, "Opechancanough, by his great age, and the fatigues of war was now grown so decrepit, that he was not able to walk alone, but was carried about by his men wherever he had a mind to move. His flesh was all macerated, his sinews slackened, and his eyelids became so heavy, that he could not see, but as they were lifted by his servants." In 1646, an English patrol captured Opechancanough while moving between towns. The lack of resistance seems to indicate that Opechancanough expected capture.

Sir William Berkeley, governor of Virginia in 1646, brought Opechancanough as "prisoner to Jamestown, where, by the governor's command, he was treated with all the respect and tenderness imaginable." This final image of the aged chief remarks on his prestige and respect even among the three generations of English settlers who feared the mighty chief. This respect only went so far, as a settler shot the imprisoned Opechancanough in the back, in the Jamestown jail.

For 100 years, Opechancanough fought for his way of life; potentially taken to Spain as a teenager, learning the ways of the Spanish, returning to his homeland, and using subterfuge to destroy his enemies in the three major conflicts of 1609, 1622, and 1644.

Don Luís traveled to Spain and returned to the Chesapeake. After feigning conversion, he and several warriors betrayed and simultaneously slew the Jesuits. (Archive Photos/ Getty Images)

ENGLISH COMMANDERS

Before the first settlers arrived at Jamestown, they had already bickered, fought, and imprisoned each other on board their ships *Godspeed*, *Susan Constant*, and the *Discovery*. Leadership at Jamestown remained contentious for the first century of English settlement. During the critical early years, basic sustainment and pressure from native tribes placed many different leaders at the head of the faltering colony.

The Virginia Company intended for a few leading men to act as the "Council of Virginia." This council elected a company president and ruled the settlement. In 1607, each of the first council members had served in prior English conflicts. Experiences in the Low Countries, Ireland, or the East encouraged these men to travel to Virginia in search of new adventures and wealth. The first wave of settlers did not intend to develop new forms of government or long-lasting colonies.

Adventurous men set sail from England many times during the Elizabethan era. Sometimes called "Elizabethan Sea Dogs," adventurers and their crew notoriously engaged the Spanish across the Caribbean, even raiding the Iberian Peninsula. Under the new reign of King James I, the Virginia Company can be seen as New World colonization, joint-stock company expansion, or governmental experimentation, but placing Jamestown and the Virginia Company among adventures of English Sea Dogs helps to portray the motivation and type of men who first came to the shores of the Chesapeake.

During the first two attempts of an English colony at Roanoke, the ships' captains who peacefully dropped off English settlers strayed during their return voyage to specifically prey on Spanish targets on the way home. Settling in Virginia enabled the same targeting. The famous defeat of the Spanish Armada remained fresh in English minds at the turn of the 17th century. Under King James I, new opportunities existed to push back the boundary of the "Spanish Main." The Coast of Virginia lay just beyond the reach of Spanish vessels and Spaniards stationed in the Caribbean or Florida Peninsula. English adventurers hoped to capitalize on their proximity to Spanish lands for theft of Spanish gold and silver. The allure of defeating a great "Indian" people spoke to the English desire of surpassing Spain. The Spanish conquistadors spent two generations exploring and conquering Central and South America. The English hoped to become new conquerors of the northern portion of the continent. A military defeat of a wealthy population could jump start English colonization.

Under King James I, the colony functioned as the Virginia Company, taking orders from the charter members of the joint-stock company. The multiple avenues of pressure applied on the Virginia colony, coupled with the high mortality and illness in the New World, created a revolving door of English leadership. In Jamestown, agendas and alliances begun by one leader rarely carried to the next. Powhatan chiefs identified this and with each change in leadership anticipated less control and authority from the subsequent leader. The several men who gained legitimate and full control of the colony each left major impacts on the English endeavor in the New World.

The 17th-century Atlantic developed into an interconnected world where English adventurers sought personal and national glory. This 1589 map depicts the travels of Sir Francis Drake during his 1586 voyage. (Buyenlarge/Getty Images)

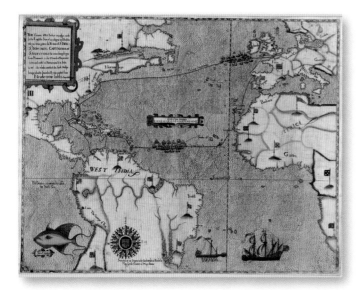

John Smith of Lincolnshire

Four centuries later, John Smith remains a household name of the Western World; not for his exploits as a Dutch mercenary or his duels against Ottoman lords but for his success in keeping the Jamestown settlement alive from 1607 to 1609 and the many works he published advocating for the Virginia colony. John Smith did not fight in the first and second Anglo-Powhatan wars, but his actions in 1607–09 contributed to the Powhatan view of Englishmen and settlement growth across the region.

In the 1590s, John Smith had left home to serve in France. His time there ended unexpectedly when his patron ran out of money. He transferred to the Austrian army where he fought in battles of the "long war" against the Ottomans. These experiences built a repertoire of soldiering seen by many of the men who accompanied the first voyage of the Virginia Company. John Smith knew how to fight, march, lead men, as well as interact with unfamiliar cultures. Smith

Formed as a join-stock company the charter members of the Virginia Company proudly advanced the English Empire. (Bettmann/ Getty Images)

claims that a Turkish noblewoman hoped to coax Smith into marrying her and serve as a converted Turkish nobleman. Smith refused and eventually made his way back to England.

Smith's military and worldly experience led the Virginia Company to appoint him as a member of the Jamestown council. On board the vessels, Smith clashed with the other appointed leaders as the only non-gentlemen of the leadership, and they imprisoned Smith on board. Upon landing at Jamestown, the council released Smith as an appointed member of the council but undermined his influence at every turn. The early days of the landing at Jamestown saw much disagreement. Fed up with poor decision making and inadequate planning Smith set out on his own authority to explore the region, hoping to find the minerals the Virginia Company sought, the Northwest Passage, or an "Indian Kingdom" worth conquering.

In the fall of 1607, Chief Opechancanough led a small party to capture Smith and his two-man party. Pamunkey warriors killed the others recognizing

Spain rose to great wealth after the conquest of the Aztecs and Incas, followed by extensive resource extraction across the continents. England stood by jealously. This 1898 depiction can be found in Georg Weber's *Allgemeine Weltgeschichte*. (Grafissimo/Getty Images)

This woodcut, first printed in 1612 with John Smith's *Map of Virginia*, was enlarged in 1630 for the publishing of Smith's biography titled *True Travels*. (Stock Montage/Getty Images)

Near the end of his life John Smith published a biography of all his travels. (Bettmann/Getty Images)

Smith as the leader. Opechancanough questioned Smith: the first question asked by the Powhatan war chief, as recorded in John Smith's *A True Relation*, was, "*Casa cunnack, peya quagh acquintan uttasantasough*," meaning, "in how many days will there come hither any more English ships?" Opechancanough knew the Englishmen's greatest strength. For the next two months the war chief led Smith on a journey up and down the Powhatan kingdom, showing him how vast and wealthy it was. John Smith quickly learned of Opechancanough's power and understanding. He recognized that a conquistador scenario where the English could ride out and crush a kingdom and steal their gold could not happen in Virginia. Smith saw that if the English settlement was to survive it would need an alliance with the Powhatans. Luckily, the Powhatans felt the same way.

The historian James Horn believes the multi-week traveling done by John Smith and Chief Opechancanough ritualistically inducted Smith as a weroance. The confederacy already contained several different people groups and loosely expected them to obey. Smith as a weroance of the English tribe differed little from that of the independent Chickahominy or the Rappahannocks within the Powhatan Confederacy.

The infamous "execution" of John Smith, where Chief Powhatan's daughter Pocahontas intervened on Smith's behalf, can be described as a death and name change common among Algonquian men. In Smith's *Generall Historie* he writes:

> Two dayes after, Powhatan having disguised himselfe in the most fearefull manner he could, caused Capt. Smith to be brought forth to a great house in the woods, and there upon a mat by the fire to be left alone… then Powhatan more like a devill then a man… came unto him and told him now they were friends, and presently he should goe to James towne, to send him two great gunnes, and a grynd-stone, for which he would give him the Country of Capahowosick, and for ever esteeme him as his sonne Nantaquoud.

Chief Powhatan granted Smith full weroance status as a subordinate tribe within the confederacy, even renaming him as a son with a new name. The land Chief Powhatan gave to Smith formerly belonged to the Paspahegh tribe. If Smith remained in Jamestown, he fulfilled this role and kept a peace between the peoples. John Smith's personal alliance with Chief Powhatan established a lasting place for the wayward Englishmen.

The alliance established by Smith protected the floundering settlement from December 1607 to October 1609. During that time, Smith relied on his experience as a mercenary soldier to barter and force his way to extract necessary food from

THE
TRUE TRAVELS, ADVENTVRES,
AND
OBSERVATIONS
OF
Captaine Ioᴛɴ Smɪᴛʜ,
In *Europe, Aſia, Affrica*, and *America*, from *Anno Domini* 1593. to 1629.

His Accidents and Sea-fights in the Straights; his Service and Stratagems of warre in *Hungaria, Tranſilvania, Wallachia*, and *Moldavia*, againſt the *Turks*, and *Tartars*; his three ſingle combats betwixt the *Chriſtian* Armie and the *Turks*.

After how he was taken priſoner by the *Turks*, ſold for a Slave, ſent into *Tartaria*; his deſcription of the *Tartars*, their ſtrange manners and cuſtomes of Religions, Diets, Buildings, Warres, Feaſts, Ceremonies, and Living; how hee ſlew the Baſhaw of *Nalbritt* in *Cambia*, and eſcaped from the *Turks* and *Tartars*.

Together with a continuation of his generall Hiſtory of *Virginia, Summer-Iles, New England*, and their proceedings, ſince 1624. to this preſent 1629; as alſo of the new Plantations of the great River of the *Amazons*, the Iles of Sᵗ. *Chriſtopher, Mevis*, and *Barbados* in the *Weſt Indies*.

All written by actuall Authours, whoſe names you ſhall finde along the Hiſtory.

LONDON,
Printed by *J. H.* for *Thomas Slater*, and are to bee ſold at the Blew Bible in *Greene Arbour*. 1630.

the neighboring villages and maintain his standing among the quarreling English. Powhatan and English formal relations stated peace, but the decentralized nature of the Powhatan tribes and the expansion-minded Englishmen resulted in theft and raids between the two peoples. With the arrival of hundreds of new settlers in the third supply, the English attempted to build forts and homesteads farther away from Jamestown. Each newly established English dwelling caused diplomatic headaches for John Smith. Smith spent his remaining months visiting Chief Powhatan and other local chiefs to keep peace and trade goods flowing to Jamestown. When an explosion severely burned Smith's body the leadership of the colony passed suddenly to George Percy. The allied "son" of Powhatan left, causing the chief to force the English "tribe" back into line.

Upon Smith's return to England, he spent the rest of his life advocating for English colonization. Smith visited New England once, but never returned to Virginia. His many published works coaxed many settlers to make the crossing and inspired further investments in the colony.

Based on the original woodcut from Smith's *Generall Historie*, this iconic scene is a ritualistic name change ceremony, not a scene of lovers. (mikroman6/Getty Images)

George Percy of Northumberland
Born the eleventh and sickly child of Henry Percy, 8th Earl of Northumberland, George Percy grew up as an unsuccessful and extra son of an important noble family. Attending various schools, Percy then joined military campaigns in Holland. He heard of the Virginia adventure and signed up hoping to make a name for himself and have improved health in the supposedly warmer climate of Virginia. As the adventure unfolded, Percy found himself repeatedly in the center of the action. He often served beyond his capacity and struggled to lead the raucous men of Virginia. Percy spent five years in Virginia as one of the few gentlemen to survive from first landing in 1607 to a departure of his choosing in 1612. As a gentleman, Percy found himself often in the leadership councils. As many others died or abandoned the colony he acted as governor three times: during the winters of 1609 and 1610, and then again in summer 1611. After disease and violence ended many lives in Jamestown, Percy left a mark through his inept persistence. Returning to England in 1612, he wrote the best alternate narrative to Smith's extensive writings of Virginia.

With John Smith's sudden departure in October 1609, Percy found himself as the newly voted president of the colony. Percy lacked the innovation and drive demonstrated by John Smith. Most historians believe that Percy and the other English leadership did not understand the accidental alliance Smith had found himself in. With the arrival of the second supply the previous

George Percy's signature. (mikroman6/Getty Images)

Portrait of George Percy.
(The Print Collector via
Getty Images)

year, Smith and Captain Newport had "crowned" Chief Powhatan as subservient chief to the King of England. The Englishmen expected Powhatan to obey their wishes while Chief Powhatan expected the Englishmen to honor his wishes. Without Smith, Percy failed to establish a new relationship with Chief Powhatan, leading to the "starving time" in the winter of 1609. Chief Powhatan and Opechancanough personally led the siege of Jamestown, lasting from November 1609 to March 1610. Under Percy's leadership a majority of the colony starved to death while trapped inside the siege.

With the relief of Thomas Gates and De La Warr's arrival, Percy fell into a subordinate role, yet led several of the skirmishes of 1610. Upon De La Warr's departure in March 1611, Percy again assumed command of Jamestown. This time the colony was well supplied and endured a few more besieged months at Jamestown until Thomas Dale arrived in May 1611 to take command. Percy's command of the besieged survivors remained weak. Dale later accused Percy of allowing the settlers to "bowl in the streets" instead of fighting back against the Powhatans.

Percy's best qualities emerged upon his return to England. Departing April 22, 1612, Percy spent five years to the day in Jamestown. Back in England, Percy wrote down his perspective of the first five years of the Jamestown colony. His account provides the most details of Smith's fights with the gentlemen and the horrific conditions endured during the starving times and subsequent conflict.

Lord Thomas West, Baron De La Warr

John Smith learned on the job; his personal experience dictated his leadership style and his reckless but effective actions. Percy's courtier background benefited the colony eventually but limited its options during the colony's first conflict. Lord Thomas West, Baron De La Warr, knew war and leadership. A member of parliament and a veteran of the English Army, De La Warr received an appointment from the Virginia Company in 1609 as governor-for-life and captain-general of Virginia. In 1610, Thomas West came to the shores of Virginia ready to turn the tide in favor of the Virginia Company.

In May 1610, the Jamestown colony had 91 settlers, a population collapse from 400 prior to the Powhatan siege. Miraculously the officers of the *Sea Venture*, the flagship of the third supply lost at sea, appeared off the Virginia coast in two hand-built vessels which had sailed from Bermuda. Despite this miracle, Dale, Gates, Newport, and Somers agreed with Percy that the emaciated survivors, lack of supplies, and Powhatan hostility dictated a withdrawal from the Jamestown colony. Dale and the healthiest members readied the survivors to depart. On June 10, 1610, all members of the Jamestown colony had boarded their small boats and awaited the ebb of the lower tide to depart Virginia. In that moment De La Warr appeared in the bay with three supply ships, settlers, and veteran soldiers to rebuild the colony. De La Warr immediately instituted martial law and began rigidly running the colony.

The Jamestown colony was mere hours away from another lost colony scenario. If De La Warr's fleet had arrived moments later, it would have found an abandoned fort on the edge of the James River. But it found the departing vessels, and on De La Warr's authority ordered all settlers back to Jamestown.

In 1608 and 1609 Smith held the colony together through politics. In 1609 and 1610, Percy convinced survivors to keep going; but in late 1610, De La Warr marched fully armored veteran English soldiers ashore at Jamestown prepared for a war fully backed by the English people. The Virginia Company through the king's support empowered De La Warr to avenge English deaths and civilize the region. As historian J. Frederick Fausz describes, "De La Warr and Lieutenant Governor Gates assigned all adult males to military companies and work parties of fifty men each, commanded by hand-picked veterans of England's Catholic conflicts. In mid-June, the governor instituted the first installment of the *Lawes Divine, Morall and Martiall*, a comprehensive, coercive legal code for promoting civil discipline, political stability." De La Warr now commanded the settlement through martial law.

Appointed governor-for-life of the Virginia Company, De La Warr personally governed the colony in 1611. (Sepia Times/ Universal Images Group via Getty Images)

To avenge the deaths of the previous year, West and his veterans brought tactics, previously seen in the Irish wars, against the Powhatan peoples. Battles in the Irish wars spanned over 150 years. English commanders in Ireland focused on chasing, trapping, and destroying enemy platoons or key villages to deter the next raid. Thomas West as captain-general orchestrated his subordinate commanders to move in companies of 50 by boat to attack and destroy Powhatan villages. De La Warr's movement by water and rapid strike techniques shaped Virginian violence for a century.

Remaining in Virginia for only one year, De La Warr returned to England to recover from scurvy and malaria. The strategies and extremely strict military law he established saved Jamestown from its lowest point in the summer of 1610 and developed military experiences that defined Virginian and Powhatan interactions for the rest of the 17th century.

De La Warr's fleet arrived just in time to save Jamestown. (Pobytov/Getty Images)

Sir Thomas Dale of Surrey

As the young colony grew stronger roots, Thomas Dale arrived, in a sense, as the second John Smith. Dale brought energy, leadership, and sound military experience to the mixed crowd of gentlemen and soldiers. Landing at Jamestown in May 1611, alongside Thomas Gates' military reinforcements for the war, Dale's nebulous background featured military service in several campaigns for the Dutch Princes since 1588. This lengthy career placed Dale among Prince Henry's and Earl Robert Cecil's favored retinue. Cecil encouraged Dale's appointment as the deputy-governor and marshal of Virginia.

Dale rose through the ranks during Leicester's expedition to the Low Countries in 1589. At some point during the campaign, he gained a captaincy and the associated gentleman's status. Dale next appeared in 1594 as one of 19 captains under consideration for promotion in Ireland. By 1598 Dale fought in France as a captain of the Earl of Southampton. Together they hurried back to Ireland to fight in the Earl of Essex's campaign of 17,000 English soldiers against Irish rebels. During this campaign Dale fought, recruited, and commanded alongside Thomas Gates and Thomas West (De La Warr). With the eventual failure of the campaign and the execution of the Earl of Essex each of these men sought new ventures to restore their reputations.

After the failed campaign in Ireland, Dale lost his command in the English army and found a new command in the Dutch armies in 1603. By 1606 he referred again to Thomas Gates as a "companion-in-arms." During the wars in the Low Countries, Dale received a knighthood. The on-and-off conflicts between the Dutch and the Spanish increased Dale's experience until the Virginia Company invited Dale to serve as the marshal for the growing colony.

The early failures at Jamestown from 1609 to 1611 motivated the Virginia Company and James I to support an intentional military campaign to Virginia in 1611. With Dale's high level of military professionalism, he trained and fully armored English companies for battle with the Powhatans. Upon the conclusion of the first Anglo-Powhatan conflict in 1614, Dale requested appointment elsewhere. He departed Jamestown in 1616 as a marshal of the East India Trading Company, dying in India in 1619.

Sir Samuel Argall of Kent

A gentleman and trained seaman, Samuel Argall first sailed with the third supply to Virginia in 1609. Navigating one of the nine vessels which departed in the third supply, Argall helped Captain Newport sail a more direct route for Virginia never previously attempted by English seamen. Argall successfully completed the journey from England to Virginia in nine weeks; a breakthrough sailing route compared to the previous record of 12 weeks and an average of 18 weeks.

Argall's new sailing route enabled him after the third supply to return to England, and sail again to Virginia for the miraculous rendezvous on June 10, 1610, which saved the colony from abandonment. Argall made a third return trip to England for the colony, returning in September 1610. As winter set in, Argall began sailing about the Chesapeake seeking friendlier tribes to trade for food. During the winter of 1610–11, Argall made many personal alliances and trade networks with tribes farther from the Jamestown settlement. By spring of 1611 Argall departed for England with the ailing De La Warr. In July 1612, Argall set sail again for Virginia on the newly

English soldiers brought tactics from various foreign wars to Virginia. This 1581 Paris conflict depicts the evolving tactics of the age. (Photo by Culture Club/Getty Images)

acquired 130-ton vessel *The Treasure*. Navigating *The Treasure*, Argall broke his own record, making it from England to Virginia in 57 days, just over eight weeks. He wintered again at Jamestown and again conducted negotiations and trade with various Chesapeake tribes.

The Anglo-Powhatan conflict reached a stalemate in 1612 and 1613 as each side realized they lacked the strength to fully destroy the other. Back in England the Virginia Company faced a backlash for its strict policies in controlling the Jamestown settlers and the high loss of life and profits it faced during the war; no new soldiers or supplies departed for the colony.

Captains Argall and Newport relied on their own negotiations to develop trading relationships separate from John Smith and Jamestown. These relationships paid off during the capture of Pocahontas and the sieges of the Second Anglo-Powhatan War. (DeAgostini/Getty Images)

Argall's experiences from two winters trading and negotiating with Powhatan and other Algonquian tribes presented him with an opportunity. While bartering with Japssus, weroance of Pasptanzie, the chief mentioned to Argall that Powhatan's daughter, Pocahontas, was visiting the tribe. Argall convinced the chief to assist him in capturing Pocahontas. With Powhatan's favored daughter captive in Jamestown, Thomas Dale and Samuel Argall brought an end to the First Anglo-Powhatan War with the marriage of Pocahontas to John Rolfe. Marriage worked as a way toward peace for both cultures.

Argall sailed many more voyages for the colony and the company, eventually serving as Jamestown's deputy governor. Argall's innovative leadership helped the colony transition from martial law to civil governance in 1617. After sailing and fighting in Algiers, Argall received a knighthood in 1622. With the dissolution of the Virginia Company in 1624 he sat on the Mandeville Commission to reorganize the colony from a joint-stock charter to a Royal Charter. On the commission, Argall competed for appointment as the first royal governor. Failing to gain the appointment he later died at sea leading an expedition to raid Cadiz in 1626.

George Yeardley of Surrey

Little is known about George Yeardley prior to his arrival in Jamestown. Yeardley came ashore at the Jamestown settlement as a hand-selected guardsman of Thomas Gates and the rest of the delayed yet surviving third supply in May 1610. The destitute colonists and crumbling settlement presented a bleak future for the colony, but Yeardley, Gates, and others took up leadership roles as best they could to save the English dream. Yeardley served Jamestown well, acting as the captain of the guard of Jamestown Fort and later as Thomas Dale's deputy at his plantation, and as deputy governor of the colony.

Yeardley held the fort when Dale left in 1616. Dale's departure spurred the Chickahominy, an independent tribe never fully allied with the English or the Powhatans, to question all previous negotiations with Dale. They claimed that he personally held the alliances intact. Yeardley's six years of experience in Jamestown enabled him to personally go to the Chickahominy tribe and convince them that Dale represented Jamestown and that all agreements would still be upheld under his leadership.

As the Spanish and Dutch did before them, the English invested in large overseas trading fleets. This 1601 illustration depicts the first sailing of the East India Trading Company fleet leaving Woolwich. (duncan1890/Getty Images)

Depicting the tools and armor of the mid-17th century, reenactors stand ready for guests to enter the replica of Jamestown Fort. (Joe Sohm/Visions of America/Getty Images)

Yeardley represents a rare English leader who quickly understood which steps to take to maintain good alliances with Powhatan and other surrounding tribes. Samuel Argall's arrival shortly after would challenge the unstable deals and alliances with indigenous tribes. The tribes of Virginia never grew comfortable with the revolving door of leaders in Jamestown. In 1617 Yeardley returned to England.

By the fall of 1618, the Virginia Company reached out to Yeardley to invite him back as the new governor of the colony. Now married to another former Jamestown settler, Temperance Flowerdew, Yeardley represented the full package of an experienced English adventurer with success and a family. Times shifted in Jamestown; in 1618 the colony no longer hung by a thread for survival but had found its stride as a tobacco plantation and a consumer of Caribbean goods. The Virginia Company commissioned Yeardley to return to Jamestown as its governor, taking with him major changes. Yeardley delivered and instituted the Great Charter, which introduced several reforms including the head-right system. To solve labor shortages, this system promised fifty acres of land for each passage purchased to Virginia. It also called for the founding of the Indian College and an order to end martial law in 1619. By 1624, despite shifting to a royal colony, Yeardley maintained the Great Charter and continued the first self-ruling assembly in the New World.

Each of these changes caused extreme ripple effects for the small colony. The head-right system incentivized importation of people. Indentured servants from England started as an easy source but when that labor pool thinned out servants and slaves from Africa became the most readily available source of labor. The head-right system provided labor and land to large plantation owners and a hope for an American dream to wayward English colonists. The Indian College, led by an energetic missionary named George Thorpe, tapped into the English desire to convert the Virginia tribes to Christianity. The college became a contentious obstacle in the second Anglo-Powhatan conflict. The formal end of martial law moved the colony toward eventual peace and instituted the first form of democratic self-governance in North America. George Yeardley, with his experience with the colony and the Powhatan tribes, instituted the major changes of the Great Charter.

With the several years of peace from 1614 to 1622, Yeardley capitalized on what can be called the first American boom. The rising price of tobacco created a product for Virginia that massively outsold its labor value. This high rate of return enabled Virginian settlers to purchase items from the Caribbean and England. Soaring prices disincentivized diversity of crops and Virginia planters doubled down on tobacco. This increased profits but also increased importation of food. When the second Anglo-Powhatan conflict arose, the shortage of English cornfields weakened the English strongholds.

The prize of Yeardley's holdings, Flowerdew Hundred, on the south bank of the James River, grew into a formidable fort and became one of the few surviving plantations after the devastating 1622 attacks. In 1623 and 1624, Yeardley led English offensives from his stronghold on the Flowerdew Hundred.

The leadership of Yeardley represents a different leadership from the previous military leaders. From 1609 to 1614 constant warfare brought many men to Virginia's shores but this unbalanced the population. During the time of plenty, the colony's focus shifted from survival to profits. By 1621 the population included more families and women, especially after the "brides for Jamestown" movement that brought 56 single women to the colony. Yeardley successfully transitioned the colony from a long-time war footing to settlements and plantations.

Yeardley used the time of plenty and his position as governor with a council and first elected burgesses to grow his own holdings. Due to ill health, his governorship ended in 1621, but by 1625 he had landholdings on the south side of the James River, in Jamestown, and across the bay on the eastern shore. Colony muster records show Yeardley as an early adopter of American slavery with many laborers listed in the 1625 accounts – white, black, and indigenous.

King James I, wary of the self-governing nature wrought by the Great Charter, used the extreme loss of life and property of 1622 to revoke the Virginia Company charter. James I planned to directly shape the colony but died in 1624. Charles I, crowned in March 1625, cared less how the colony ran as long as it grew. Charles I re-appointed Yeardley to the governorship in 1626. This reappointment hardened the growing tradition of representative government in Virginia. Yeardley instituted it in 1619 and eight years later gained full approval to continue the representative government laid out under the company charter.

Yeardley's leadership changed Jamestown from a floundering military outpost to a flourishing colony, pushing the traditional boundaries of representative government. The diplomacy conducted by Yeardley shaped English views of what type of relationships were possible across Virginia. After the outbreak of the Second Anglo-Powhatan War many

De La Warr, Gates, Dale, and Yeardley all served together during the failed Leinster Irish campaign. (Hulton Archive/Getty Images)

tribes defected from the Powhatan circles to maintain friendly relationships with the English. Yeardley died at 39 years of age as the royal governor of Virginia in 1627.

Francis Wyatt of Kent

Appointed colonial governor upon Yeardley's request to step down in 1621, Francis Wyatt, like many of the leading men of Virginia before him, had previously served in Holland and in the English Army in Ireland. Despite the authority of the Virginia Company's board of directors, King James I influenced the board to prevent Edwin Sandys from receiving the appointment of governor. Sandys strongly believed in Virginia, often disregarding the king's wishes for the colony in hopes of growing a stronger self-sustaining society. Wyatt acted as a bridge between the private board of directors and the king's advisers who sought to rein in the independent nature of the Virginia colony. Despite Wyatt's support of the king, he brought with him to Virginia the first written constitution for the New World. This constitution formalized many of the habits and forms of representative government used under Governor Yeardley.

Upon the outbreak of the Second Anglo-Powhatan War in 1622, Wyatt relied on his military experiences to form marches and raids against the Powhatan tribes. His success in defending the colony in the fateful year of 1622 enabled him to keep his position of governor during the change to a Royal Charter. The king hoped to remove the charter and constitution but failed to finalize the plans before his death. Yeardley returned in 1626 as the governor with King Charles I's approval to continue the constitution of 1621. Wyatt and Yeardley worked together for several years to militarily secure the Virginia colony. In 1626, Wyatt returned to his family plantations in Ireland.

In 1639, Francis Wyatt came to Virginia to serve as the royal governor for a second time. His arrival in 1639 found a completely different colony than when he had left in 1626. The colony had waged continual war from 1622 to 1632. The head-right system brought thousands of English indentured servants to its shore, supplemented by hundreds of captured black laborers from central Africa. Each transported person gave landowners the right to more land and more land gave the owner greater influence in the House of Burgesses. Excluding the third and final ambush of Opechancanough in 1644, the 1640s ushered in a new era of complete English dominance of the region. Dominance led to political debates and strain, less between English and Powhatan and more between English classes of landowner, tenant, free laborer, servant, and slave.

Several years of agricultural failure turned Virginians to John Rolfe's Orinoco Tobacco, which coincided with an Atlantic boom in tobacco, bringing great wealth to the Virginia area. Artwork by Sydney King for the National Park Service. (MPI/Getty Images)

John Harvey of Dorset

Governor John Harvey acted as the last English commander bearing a significant impact on the second Anglo-Powhatan conflict. The Harvey family line remains largely unknown, but most historians believe Harvey's family rose to wealth through trade, most likely in silk. John Harvey personally procured food for King James I's household in the 1610s. Under King Charles, Harvey served as a merchant sea captain and a naval commander.

While transporting goods to and from London, the Virginia Company granted him land in Virginia hoping to encourage his return trips to the colony. This led to Harvey investing heavily in the Virginia Company. His seasonal arrival at Jamestown represented one of the major tobacco exports each year. His own land also cultivated tobacco. Harvey relied on his experience in logistics from the king's court to the Atlantic to maximize profits and influence. By 1628 he had attracted the attention of the royal bureaucrats who wanted to increase Jamestown's profits.

Ongoing battles in the Low Countries kept English men of war continually well trained in the latest military art. (Culture Club/Getty Images)

Harvey arrived in Virginia as its newest royal governor in 1629, beginning a new administration in 1630 which saw many reforms and bureaucratic adjustments to improve the colony. The long-time landowners of the colony reported Harvey as a quick-tempered and demanding leader, blaming his years as a sea captain for his aggressive attitude toward other leaders of the colony. Despite pushback from the gentlemen of the colony, Harvey developed Jamestown's prosperity. He finally settled the peace with Opechancanough in 1632 and built a palisade wall from the James River to the York River in 1634, creating a walled-off territory encompassing half of the Virginia Peninsula, nearly 200 square miles. The increased focus on farming enabled more livestock and corn to grow in English territory. Harvey successfully prevented the king from monopolizing tobacco, keeping the landowners of Virginia pleased despite his aggressive dealings with them.

Harvey has many similarities to Samuel Argall. He did not portray the same charismatic leadership as Argall, but he relied on experience as a sea captain and merchant to find ways to negotiate with Chief Opechancanough and recalcitrant landowners. As an outsider compared to Yeardley or Francis, Harvey avoided the grudges of the past and focused on what changes could most benefit Jamestown and the growing colony.

The mercantile system implemented by the European colonizers often prevented manufacture in the New World. The Virginia colony received little royal oversight enabling it to pursue ironworks, shipbuilding, and glass making. (MPI/Getty Images)

OPPOSING FORCES

POWHATAN WAY OF WAR

The Powhatan Confederacy contained several different tribal groups, yet each group fell into the broader category of an Eastern Woodland Algonquian tribe. Such tribes lived on the east side of the Appalachians, built sedentary villages, and spoke a dialect of the Algonquian language group. Along the Chesapeake and the rivers of Virginia also lay Siouan and Iroquoian peoples. Among these tribes, common forms of warfare developed.

The Algonquian tribes relied on a peace chief for all negotiations and directions of the tribe and a war chief for all forceful events. The peace chief superseded the war chief but, as demonstrated by the Powhatan tribes, the war chief's influence increased during prolonged war. For the Powhatan Confederacy, when the chief-of-chiefs, or Mamanatowick, agreed to a war, the war chief gathered the allied war chiefs to form war parties. War parties ranged from a raiding squad of five to ten warriors to an army of 800 men.

The Powhatan Confederacy had large populations of women and children but disproportionately few men of fighting age. Smith notes this several times, although well aware of the capabilities of a smaller tribe to overwhelm Jamestown. In Smith's *Generall Historie* he states, "Within 60 myles of James Towne, there are about some 5,000 people, but of able men fit for their warres scarce 1,500… Six or seaven hundred have beene the most hath beene seene together." Smith's assessment proved true in the ensuing conflicts. Historian J. Frederick Fausz estimates that the consolidation of the Powhatan Confederacy could have theoretically fielded a population of 1,470 warriors during the First Anglo-Powhatan War, a threatening number compared to Jamestown's paucity of 90 Englishmen in 1610 and near 200 in 1611. The 1622 Massacre revealed the limits of the fielded army as the various points simultaneously hit on the day of the massacre required over 1,200 warriors to execute. This limit perhaps saved Jamestown and the other fortified settlements when Powhatan raiding teams refused to mass and attack a fortified settlement.

Powhatan Tactics
The raiding culture of Algonquian tribes can be called guerrilla warfare, but that term does not fully appreciate the organization of the Powhatan Confederacy. Powhatans raided frequently, and they raided enemies far to the north or west as well as among neighbors. Allegiance to the confederacy did

protect tribes from raids but several nearby tribes remained outside of Chief Powhatan's hierarchy, such as the Chickahominy. Annually Powhatan tribes raided the Monacans upriver of modern-day Richmond. The Massawomacks in the vicinity of the Potomac River posed the greatest threat to the Powhatan tribes as they rowed birch-bark canoes compared to Powhatan dugout canoes.

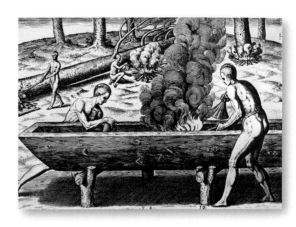

The Massawomacks conducted lightning raids, striking in the early morning, and raced north quicker than any Powhatan oarsman could follow; a culture of raiding made for warriors who excelled at quick quiet movement through the Virginia woods. At least one war chief led a raiding party, and the raid always served a single purpose. A raid could be burning crops, capturing women and children, destroying watercraft, poisoning water or food sources, stealing high-value items, stealing food, or assassinating a leader. These types of raids are common to many tribal societies, but the Powhatan system of peace chief and war chief created a tribal dialogue before forceful events took place. A leadership agreement to conduct raids demonstrated a planning organization greater than those found in less-consolidated societies.

The Powhatans followed Algonquian traditions of dugout canoe manufacturing, burning and chipping out large tree trunks. These heavy yet durable canoes plied Chesapeake waters despite English dominance of the rivers. This 1590 engraving is by Theodor de Bry. (Hulton Archive/Getty Images)

Powhatan warriors carried a bow with a club slung over one shoulder to hang on their back. When beginning combat, every member of a formation would fire his arrows first. A few warriors protected the flanks, but this would be a small number as the main body intended to inundate an enemy with arrows. Pamunkeys especially honored archery. Many accounts discuss the Pamunkey system where a bowman slung a quiver off his hip, stuffed full of arrows, and carried even more arrows in his bow hand and even his mouth. As John Smith describes in his *Map of Virginia*:

Powhatans feared the Monacans and Massawomacks more than the English, a point often exploited by English negotiators. This 1591 work by Theodor de Bry depicts an attack on a Florida tribe, but the same dilemmas faced the tribes of Virginia. (Art Images via Getty Images)

> For fishing, hunting, and warres they use much their bow and arrowes. They bring their bowes to the forme of ours by the scraping of a shell. Their arrowes are made some of straight young sprigs, which they head with bone, some 2 or 3 ynches long… Another sort of arrowes they use made of Reeds. These are peeced with wood, headed with splinters of christall, or some sharpe stone, the spurres of a Turkey, or the bill of some bird.

Smith continues to describe how a Powhatan hunter carried extra arrow tips in a bracer on his wrist so he could make an arrow on the move. In the village, Powhatans made a glue from the boiled jelly of antlers, which would "not dissolve in cold water." Powhatans easily made bows and arrows for all uses.

Powhatan warriors also carried "targets" and "swords." Clubs ranged from a carved wooden mallet to a bone sword with copper embedded along the cutting edge. Powhatans used and molded copper well before English settlement. Smith writes the most common "sword" was a "sword of wood [worn] at

This woodcut printed for John Smith in 1612 depicts the size of the Powhatan bows. (mikroman6/Getty Images)

their backs … [with] the horne of a Deere put through a peece of wood in forme of a Pickaxe [known in the Powhatan language as a *tockahack*]."

"Targets" were shaped from tree bark reinforced with sticks and reeds to form a circle or oval shape. Warriors often carried the bow and target with the wooden sword slung on their backs. Smith describes these weapons in his writings. All Powhatan warriors carried smaller cutting weapons such as a stone or bone knife. As European trade flourished, Powhatan people quickly included hatchets, European knives, and swords into their arsenals. Powhatan clubmen also carried a small "target" or buckler shield of tightly woven bark and branches.

In combat the initial role of a clubman was to guard the archers from ambush. Placed on the wings or to the rear of the archers, a few guards protected the formation. Archers acted as the main element of an engagement, intending to harry and drop an enemy who could be finished when the formation advanced. The larger the attacking element the more intentionally archers formed a crescent shape to envelop enemies with arrow volleys. During his capture in December 1607, Smith found his comrade Jehu Robinson dead with 30 arrows in him. The size of the English force did not call for use of equivalent force; the entire company of archers loosed arrows on two Englishmen. Once enemies routed or came too close, clubmen stood ready to counterattack and move into a village to burn or capture it.

The Chesapeake tribes highly valued archery skills. Prior to declaring war, opposing men could meet to discuss options. An archery competition occasionally acted as a determination of who had more spiritual power and favor. Wicker and wooden shields a short distance away became targets for the chosen archer. According to the writings of George Percy, the English experienced this when a party of 40 warriors came to the outskirts of Jamestown and asked to stay the night in the fort. The English refused but some men came outside the fort to camp and discuss with the group. He writes that during the evening:

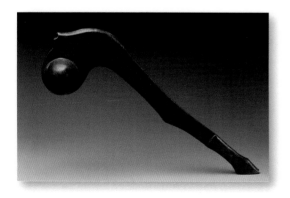

Powhatan war clubs ranged from carved wood to wood with inlaid copper teeth. (The Charles and Valerie Diker Collection of Native American Art, The Metropolitan Museum of Art, 2017)

One of our Gentlemen having a target [shield] which he trusted in … set it up against a tree, willing one of the Savages to shoot; who took from his back an arrow of an ell [1¼ yards] long, drew it strongly in his bow, and shot the target a foot through, or better: which was strange, being that a pistol could not pierce it. We seeing the force of his bow, afterwards set him up a steel target; he shot again, and burst his arrow all to pieces. He presently pulled out another arrow, and bit it in his teeth, and seemed to be in a great rage; so he went away in great anger. Their bows are made of tough hasell [hazel wood], headed with very sharp stones, and are made artificially like a broad arrow.

Percy reveals the frustration felt by the Powhatan war party as their machismo and challenges were shattered alongside an arrow.

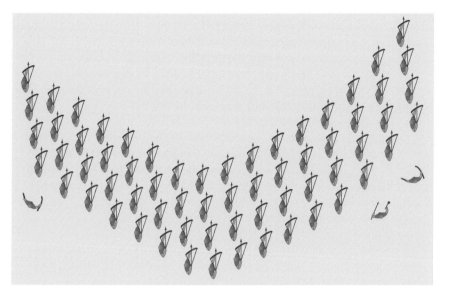

This illustration of four rows of men, followed by two chiefs and a priest, depicts a Powhatan company as described by John Smith during his captivity in 1607. Tribes of the Powhatan Confederacy fought in organized crescent moon formations. The formation volleyed, charged, re-formed, and volleyed again by the command of the nearby war chiefs. Powhatan engagements intended to inundate enemies with arrows then charge in to finish wounded men with war clubs. The men in formation remained spaced enough that each could volley simultaneously.

The many tribes of the Powhatan Confederacy communicated daily, developing relationships. John Smith described an extraordinary example of the Powhatan way of war, when as their prisoner he asked how they conduct war. On the spot, war chief Opechancanough called up his elder brother Opitchapam, a peace chief, to summon other warriors for a training demonstration. John Smith watched in disbelief as dozens of warriors from separate tribes arrived shortly to take part in a mock battle. Smith writes:

Having painted and disguised themselves in the fiercest manner they could devise, they divided themselves into two Companies, neare a hundred in a company. The one company called Monacans, the other Powhatans. Either army had their Captaine. These as enemies took their stands a musket shot one from another; ranked themselves 15 a breast, and each ranke from another 4 or 5 yards, not in fyle, but in the opening betwixt their fyles. So the Reare could shoot as conveniently as the Front. Having thus pitched the fields: from either part went a messenger with these conditions, that whosoever were vanquished, such as escape upon their submission in two dayes after should live, but their wives and children should be prize for the Conquerours. The messengers were no sooner returned, but they approached in their orders; On each flanke a Serjeant, and in the Reare an Officer for Lieutenant, all duly keeping their orders, yet leaping and singing after their accustomed tune, which they onely use in Warres. Upon the first flight of arrowes they gave such horrible shouts and screeches, as so many infernall hell-hounds could not have made them more terrible. When they had spent their arrowes, they joyned together prettily, charging and retyring, every ranke seconding other. As they got advantage they catched their enemies by the hayre of the head, and downe he came that was taken. His enemy with his wooden sword seemed to beat out his braines, and still they crept to the Reare, to maintaine the skirmish. The Monacans decreasing, the Powhatans charged them in the forme of a halfe Moone; they unwilling to be inclosed, fled all in a troope to their Ambuscadoes, on whom they led them very cunningly.

This powerfully portrays the methods of Algonquian warfare. Smith tells us in this mock battle that 15 Powhatan bowmen stood in a loose line with six subsequent files forming a loose square. This square fired arrows, advanced forward, fired more arrows, then clashed in a melee. For the front row a short melee ensued then broke for the next line to engage with its counterpart line. Even in training Smith saw warriors thrashed by one another.

Chief Powhatan reserved large formations for decisive events. The record tells of massed Powhatan warriors destroying towns that fell from grace. But small raids and ambushes remained the preferred method for Algonquian tribes. In Smith's *Generall Historie*, he describes two ambushes which paint the picture for Algonquian surprise attacks. "Thirty or forty of the Rappahannock, had so accommodated themselves with branches, we took them for little bushes growing among the sedge." This party of Rappahannocks rose from their hidden positions and fired arrows at the English shallop sailing upriver. Later in the same mission:

> Our sentinell saw an arrow fall by him, though we had ranged up and downe more then an houre … not seeing where a Salvage could well hide himself. Upon the alarum by that we had recovered our armes, there was about an hundred nimble Indians skipping from tree to tree, letting fly their arrows so fast as they could: the trees here served us for Baricadoes [barricades]… About halfe an houre this continued, then they all vanished as suddainly as they approached.

Both a 40-man and 100-man raiding party attempted to destroy the English expeditions. Upon the English survival the local chiefs quickly changed their tone, often negotiating and trading immediately after an ambush. These quick changes indicate that Chesapeake tribes took advantages when they had them but quickly adapted to failures.

Powhatan Towns

Powhatan villages often placed palisaded walls around the whole town. Smith's eyewitness description from 1608 describes one as a "Palisaded town, mantled with barks of trees, with scaffolds like mounts, breasted about with barks very formally." This advanced wall may have surprised European observers in 1608. "Mantled" refers to the bark tied to the palisaded logs. "Scaffolds like mounts" describes a palisade wall similar to the European method with logs tied up to create scaffolding against the wall so that a warrior could stand above the palisade to shoot an arrow. "Breasted about with barks" refers to the scaffolding, meaning that it also had bark coverings alongside of it to protect the archer. "Very formally" compliments the neatness and precision of the palisade wall with mounts. This wall was much more than a few loose logs stood on end, it had intentional defenses and firing points.

A wooden palisade wall created choke points between village sleeping areas and the approach of outsiders. Daily, men could come and go from a town to conduct hunting and canoeing activities. The wall was intended to prevent all-out raids and ensure only friendly men entered the town. These walls did not compare to wooden palisades common in Europe or early European settlements in America. Algonquian people cut trees down with stone tools, often

The town of Pomeiooc, drawn in 1590 by Theodor de Bry. It was located nearer to Florida but was similar in style to many Powhatan palisaded villages. (DeAgostini/Getty Images)

wood with quartz stone wedges. Then they would shape the wood with bone or stone implements. The difficulty of cutting down large trees caused Algonquian fortifications to be built from young, small trees. After being cut, holes were dug to embed the trees, spacing them about an arm's span apart. The subsequent gaps then received a woven pattern tied with branches, bark, and other filler items to create a barrier a man could not push through. Despite not meeting European standards for a palisade of the 16th century, these walls effectively defended towns from small-scale attacks.

This 1877 illustration portrays a 1609 battle between the Wyandots and Huron, with Samuel De Champlain fighting with the Huron. Iroquois' battles had many similarities to Algonquian Powhatans'. (The Print Collector/Print Collector/Getty Images)

As a sedentary society, crop growth defined town locations and quality of defenses. Smith and Percy both reported a mature farm could produce crop twice or even three times in a season. The fertile tidewater lands and long growing seasons contained high potential for large populations. Within a Powhatan town, storehouses dedicated to corn, wheat, tobacco, or skins preserved Powhatan peoples throughout a winter. Defending these locations predicated how firm a defense warriors would put up. A palisaded town with no, or empty, storehouses, could be abandoned. Dale, Gates, and De La Warr all reported that at times they approached a village ready for a fight but found it completely abandoned. Powhatans allowed towns to be burned to preserve their fighting strength for key positions. As Powhatans gained greater access to iron and European hatchets, they became quicker at rebuilding town sites. In the 1620s, English soldiers often burned the same towns multiple times in a campaign season.

ENGLISH WAY OF WAR

Entering the 17th century English soldiers had served in foreign armies, as border guards in Scotland, and in the long Irish wars. Englishmen had learned the evolving tactics of war mostly from the Dutch War for Independence, also known as the 80 Years' War. In the Dutch War, continental armies quickly iterated new strategies to match the changing technologies of muskets, cannons, and fortifications. Classical treatises inspired the armies of Europe to incorporate classical and Roman methods of war into modern tactics. Roman-style maniples enabled Dutch, Spanish, and German armies to experiment with battlefield control of large formations through smaller unit maneuvers. Experiments led to shrinking battalion formations, from 1,000-man formations to as low as 200 with frontages of 57 meters in some cases. Smaller units began to drill more specifically to increase their rate of fire. Drills included the counter march, turning in reverse through your own lines, and later marching to the right and left of the main body to march to a formation's rear. The high rate of experienced veterans in Virginia brought rapid adaptation of the most modern tactics. Virginian soldiers implemented snaphance muskets decades before European armies.

Accompanying the evolving formation experiments, unit compositions sought the optimum method to present forward firepower but still contain pikemen to

push an enemy melee aside. Digging and field-work fortifications grew in use seeing the rapid construction of defenses, another Roman-style development. One unit pattern used by the English in Jamestown was a company formation of muskets on the left and right and pikemen in the center. This popular Dutch formation would be known to the veterans and fulfill the open field requirements in Virginia. English soldiers brought to Virginia the creative warfare methods learned from the borders of Scotland, fields of Europe, and the high seas of the Caribbean. The harsh reality of war in Virginia brought out the border reivers and sea dogs just as frequently as the modern renaissance warrior.

English Tactics

The first wave of colonists brought mostly adventurers looking for quick exploitation of resources. After the start of the First Anglo-Powhatan War, the Virginia Company sought out military veterans for the Virginian ranks. Veterans brought modern fortifications to Virginia and experimented with new and aging armor and weapons. The Virginia Company purchased new and old equipment for the colony, stocking mismatched arms across the various settlements. Taken during the transition to a royal colony, the 1624 muster roll was a registry of every man's household and items which benefited the colony, including the exact armament stored in each settlement.

The Arms and Armor of all 19 Settlements in Virginia

Item	Qty	Item	Qty
Armor, complete	342	Pieces fixed (non-matchlock)	932
Coats of mail and head pieces	260	Snaphance pieces	49
Jackets, coats, and corselets	26	Matchlocks	47
Quilted coats and buff coats	20	Pistols	55
Pieces of ordinance	20	Powder in lbs	1,129.75
Murderers	14	Lead and shot in lbs	9,657
Petrowhels	6	Swords	429
Fauconnet	1		

The 1624 Virginia muster shows us that the men of Virginia had more than enough firearms to outfit every man in the colony, but not enough for large, uniformed formations. The many coats and mails stored in the colony enabled Englishmen to armor themselves for melee combat. Early 17th-century muskets made for better defense than offense, especially against rapid-firing Powhatan archers. English captains relied heavily on armor and melee weapons to drive Powhatans from the field. The dense Virginia woods prevented "shot" formations from being fully effective. Thus, the best picture of an English warrior in 1609 Jamestown was a Dutch veteran dressed in a buff coat, a full metal breast and backplate with attached faulds, and a metal morin-style helmet carrying a sword and a musket.

English Weapons

Pikes appeared in all European formations. Matching the Dutch and Spanish armies of the period, the pikeman was the backbone of a company formation in the first year of Jamestown. No halberds are mentioned in the muster roll but halberd heads have been found in the archeology of Jamestown and Martin's Hundred. This has suggested that the halberd and pike may have been cataloged as a more personal item and, therefore, it would have been assumed a militia-citizen would have them and not list them as company property available for company use.

Gunpowder weapons increased in every iteration of European combat in the late 16th and early 17th centuries. At the turn of the 17th century the Dutch and Spanish placed musket men on the right and left flanks of a pikeman formation. The size could scale from three small platoons all the way to large battalion formations. Musket refers to shoulder-fired weapons in the 16th and 17th centuries. Muskets at the turn of the century were heavy and required a V-shaped rest to set the weapon on. Jamestown soldiers had many weapons on site. The 1624 muster lists 932 "pieces fixed;" these were heavy harquebuses that England had unloaded on the Jamestown colony, and the local blacksmith modified them to fire more easily. Most importantly, the 1624 muster roll shows 49 snaphance pieces. Elizabeth City and James City held the snaphances. A snaphance is not a simple weapon; intended as a fowling piece but being a smoothbore musket, it could fire any shot. The weapon had several moving parts and a delicate balance to load and fire without a rest. The snaphance was lighter and more reliable than older variants. The 1624 attack on the Pamunkey village claimed three dozen musketeers fired in volleys, likely with their new snaphances. The muster roll supports this,

A snaphance musket improved the previous snaplock muskets, developing a wheel lock to more reliably hold the strike in the pan. (Gift of William H. Riggs, The Metropolitan Museum of Art, 1913)

This illustration of Jamestown depicts the fort as of 1611 as five sided and with three cannon mounts. (Artwork by Donato Spedaliere © Osprey Publishing Ltd)

showing only 49 snaphances present in the colony; thus, a platoon of three dozen men utilizing 36 snaphances fits the historical evidence.

The 1624 muster lists 41 cannons, one being a modern falconet. Of the 41 cannons, 30 were stationed in Jamestown and 16 at Elizabeth City. The heavy weaponry was intended to fend off Spanish attack, not Powhatan. One discrepancy from the muster role is that, as of 1624, many settlements had retreated to safe zones after the 1622 attack and had yet to spread back out; the density of cannons at James and Elizabeth may have to do with the withdrawal.

Jamestown Fort and Population

The fort at Jamestown, first built in 1607, occasionally burned down, allowing the defenders to improve the fort at each iteration. The fort began as three sided with half-moon shaped cannon mounts on the three corners. As the settlement grew, the fort expanded into a five-sided bulwark but kept the same three cannon mounts. The "new city" at Jamestown eventually constructed a palisade wall connecting the house just south of the fort to the fort walls. The walls stood 14 feet high.

Intended as English expansion and colonization, the population of Jamestown dictated the area of control and the numbers of fighting men. See the table for the oscillating population of Jamestown. Note that the Powhatan offenses of 1609 and 1622 align with a large English population. Each time the colony reached a new high of population and land claims, Powhatans reacted. The plotted points show the population at key known dates. It is known that 38 men survived the first winter, and the population then rose to 381 with the arrival of the third supply. A population of 90 is recorded in 1610, made up with the survivors of the starving time and the wreck of *Sea Venture* on Bermuda. In August 1611, the arrival of Gates' fleet brought the population to a new high of 752. This steadily rose to 1,600 after the arrival of the "brides for Jamestown" in early 1622. The losses of the 1622 massacre are hard to depict due to high immigration directly after the event, but the muster roll of 1624 counted 1,200 people in the colony.

Figures compiled from a variety of sources, including: Horn's *A Brave and Cunning Prince*; Schmidt's *The Divided Dominion*; Fausz's "An 'Abundance of Blood Shed on Both Sides'"; and Virginia Colony Muster and Census records (www.virtualjamestown.org/census_main.html).

Jamestown Population, 1607–24

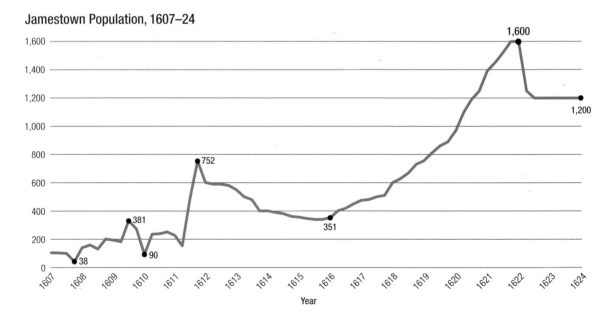

OPPOSING PLANS

The first cultural encounters between Englishmen and Powhatans produced two societies wary of each other's actions but each hoping to gain from the other. During the first few days on land in Virginia, local tribes attacked English landing parties. This willingness to jump to violence likely stemmed from the shared cultural history of Spanish encounters, particularly at the former Ajácan Mission. Once Powhatans realized the newcomers were not Spanish, their attitudes changed. English attitudes toward the Powhatans reflected their experiences with other distant peoples. Heavy-handedness in Ireland or negotiation on the high seas represent the dichotomy of English approaches.

POWHATAN GOALS

Chief Powhatan and Opechancanough took separate approaches to the English presence. From the first encounters, Chief Powhatan sought to find what the Englishmen could offer him. Powhatan intentionally brought John Smith into his sphere of influence to build alliances. Chief Powhatan's spatial awareness accepted the English settlers as long as they stayed near the spit of land they called Jamestown. The Powhatan Confederacy claimed many tribes, some who barely submitted to Chief Powhatan's rule. If the English played their expected part as a subordinate tribe, Chief Powhatan took great interest in the navigational, script, and engineering powers demonstrated by the Englishmen. Powhatan sought to understand the letters and notes exchanged between the chiefs of the English settlement. Prior to 1607, Chief Powhatan's greatest fears were the Monacans to the west and the Massawomacks to the north. Both tribal groups held a technological advantage over the Powhatans. The Monacans extracted copper and molded it as head pieces and decorative plates. The Massawomacks used lightweight canoes to raid south.

Chief Powhatan did not pursue full destruction of the Englishmen as he focused on the long-term success of his confederacy. He willingly put up with the misunderstandings and sudden acts of violence, hoping to create a better long-term future. In March of 1609, when only 38 emaciated Englishmen remained, Chief Powhatan pulled back to preserve a relationship with the outsiders who brought new vessels, new weapons, and advanced means of communication to his shores.

Opechancanough also focused on the long-term survival of his people. The future pursued by Opechancanough involved the complete destruction of the English settlements. Opechancanough believed the reports from Powhatans who traveled to England and back that an unlimited tide of Englishmen could sail to their lands. If Opechancanough is Paquiquineo, he understood the strengths and weaknesses of the Spanish and applied them to the English. Early in the exchanges, Opechancanough ingratiated himself with the English; he tended to forgive and draw closer to his enemies, waiting for the best time to overthrow them. In the first and second Anglo-Powhatan wars, Chief Powhatan and Opitchapam held Opechancanough back from all-out warfare. Chief Powhatan commanded respect as long as he lived; to our knowledge Opechancanough never overstepped his position with Chief Powhatan. The ascension of Opitchapam to the Mamanatowick position saw constant challenges from Opechancanough.

The poisoning of Opechancanough in 1623 prevented him from gaining full control over Opitchapam. Weak and ill for much of the 1620s Opechancanough's ultimate goal of removing all Europeans from the Chesapeake never happened. As the Mamanatowick, he would try again in 1644.

ENGLISH GOALS

Before setting foot in the New World, London planners sought three options in Virginia. First, conquest; if a nation like those found in Mexico or Peru existed on the North American continent English adventurers hoped to conquer it. Second, gold; the ship loads, and fleet loads of precious metals brought from the New World to Spain caused England to jealously look on. Decades of war in Ireland and the Low Countries required more funding to hire various armies and outfit English expeditions. Ultimately, England required incoming wealth from overseas. Third, trade; England's long history with far-flung international trade acted as an easy outlet after failures of conquest and mining. Regrettably for the English, none of the three options existed in the Chesapeake.

John Smith's purpose of exploration was not to find more lands to settle but richer kingdoms to conquer. The purposes of John Ratcliffe and De La Warr's fraught expeditions into the mountains were not to cut into the heart of the Powhatan Confederacy but to find mining locations to report back to London. Captain Christopher Newport and Captain Samuel Argall's many unsanctioned negotiations with tribes near and far from Jamestown all sought the singular purpose of finding a profitable trading commodity in the region.

Plantation production remained the fourth option no gentleman of the Virginia Company desired to pursue. As the expenditure increased and the death toll mounted, London planners rethought the options in the New World. Jamestown lay on a similar latitude to Spain and the Mediterranean. Planners hoped that valuable crops of the Mediterranean could be grown in the reportedly fertile Virginian soil. Sugar, silk, cotton, ginger, limes, pimento, and indigo all failed to flourish in the cold winters and wet summers of the Chesapeake.

The campaigns of the First Anglo-Powhatan War intended to secure the English foothold in the New World. The expeditions of 1610 intended to prevent a "starving time" from happening again. Every target hit in 1610 saw the theft and collection of food from the defeated tribes. Once rations were secured, the next objective became a clear line of English control. Thomas Gates expertly planned to control and defend the James River from the north and south with sporadic fortresses built at intervals along the river.

Gates realized the English naval advantage and ensured that every conquest and new settlement was supported by water.

John Rolfe played a small military role in the First Anglo-Powhatan War and died before the second, but the main target of both wars can be attributed to his ingenuity. Rolfe survived the wreck of the *Sea Venture* on Bermuda, and he brought with him pre-purchased Trinidadian tobacco seeds. Rolfe heard that a native tobacco plant grew in Virginia but was disliked by the first wave of settlers. Hoping to capitalize on the natural climate favored by the native tobacco he experimented with the sweeter Trinidadian tobacco to develop his personal strain that he called Orinoco Tobacco. The first four barrels of Virginian-grown sweet tobacco traveled on board Captain Argall's *The Treasure* along with Rolfe and his new wife Pocahontas, arriving in England in 1614. The tobacco cash crop was born.

The Second Anglo-Powhatan War became a "just war" in the eyes of the English after the 1622 Massacre. The second war predictably coincided with major land expansions and high prices of tobacco, in addition to the head-right system which rewarded landowners for importing more laborers. The March 1622 attack unleashed the English war machine to secure as much land as interested them to increase tobacco plantations and colonial defenses. Each campaign in the 1620s targeted strongpoints or fertile tobacco lands. The various English commanders benefited from the head-right system; the more laborers imported, the more land was granted directly by the Virginia Company.

English leadership did not intentionally set out to commit genocide against the Powhatan tribes, but it intentionally used heavy-handed tactics to break Powhatan will and to drive them out of plantation lands, separating themselves. The First Anglo-Powhatan War saw Irish tactics of indiscriminate killing to subdue populations, while the second conflict saw targeted starvation by destroying crops at seasonal times to prevent the tribes from having a winter food supply. This agenda caused Powhatans to either turn to the English for aid or leave the region. Some tribes did leave the region, some assimilated, and some fought to the death.

In summary, the leaders of Jamestown sought in the first war to secure a permanent foothold along the James River; in the second war they sought to increase the agricultural land and to secure their zones establishing defensive strongpoints.

The explosion in the value of tobacco during the 1610s created many plantations up and down the James River. English laborers brought by the head-right system farmed many plantations by 1620. A painting by Sydney King. (Hulton Archive/Getty Images)

THE CAMPAIGNS

FIRST ANGLO-POWHATAN WAR: 1609, SHATTERING OF FIRST-CONTACT RELATIONSHIPS

John Smith dominated the leadership of Jamestown in 1608 and 1609. Smith utilized his unique relationship with Chief Powhatan and Opechancanough to develop a stable trade relationship. Food remained the key item needed by English settlers. Initially content with minimal farming, the Virginia Company dispatched Captain Newport in the second supply with instructions to purchase food from the indigenous tribes to reduce the men's labor. London assumed that if the men spent less time farming, they could spend more time on profitable ventures.

Attempting to hold the colony together, John Smith forbade men from trading with the local tribes. Smith hoped to present one face, one leader, and one price to the tribes to maintain his standing and to build an economic system that could support continual purchases from the tribes. Captain Christopher Newport returned to the colony in summer 1609. His instructions to purchase and bribe to obtain Powhatan supplies contradicted John Smith's orders. Newport and his sailors traded freely with tribes. The newly arrived sailors paid whatever they wanted, often giving over swords and guns for a few bushels of corn. This infuriated Smith who found trading partners criticizing him for not paying as well as his "father" Newport did.

The Newport versus Smith trade relationship inflated Powhatan prices to the point that the storehouses of Jamestown could not pay. Smith, a war veteran, turned to force to maintain his position within the Powhatan hierarchy and protect the long-term survival of the colony. Smith began arriving at villages with his "good shottes," a specifically recruited band of veterans willing to force the Powhatans to trade at the lower prices. Smith even put a pistol to Opechancanough's head during an exchange. Smith himself records in his *Generall Historie* how he debated for the last time with Chief Powhatan. In their final exchange, Smith records Powhatan saying:

> Captaine Smith, I never use any Werowance so kindely as your selfe, yet from you I receive the least kindnesse of any. Captaine Newport gave me swords, copper, cloathes, a bed, towels, or what I desired; ever taking what I offered him, and would send away his gunnes when I intreated him: none doth deny

to lye at my feet, or refuse to doe what I desire, but onely you; of whom I can have nothing but what you regard not, and yet you will have whatsoever you demand. Captaine Newport you call father, and so you call me; but I see for all us both you will doe what you list, and we must both seeke to content you.

Smith replies:

Powhatan you must know, as I have but one God, I honour but one King; and I live not here as your subject, but as your friend to pleasure you with what I can. By the gifts you bestow on me, you gaine more then by trade: yet would you visit mee as I doe you, you should know it is not our custome, to sell our curtesies as a vendible commodity.

This exchange reveals a chief who is willing to work with John Smith. Yet Smith is stressed by three factors; first, he knew Gates would arrive any day, ousting him from the leadership. Second, Newport would return shortly to England, and Smith needed to force down the prices so he could keep buying food. Third, if Powhatan thought Smith was weak, the larger population of the Powhatans could overcome the English settlement. After this exchange, Powhatan slipped away, not to be seen again by the English until 1614.

With Chief Powhatan missing from the action, authority deferred to Opechancanough. Frustrated by the gentlemen and by sickness, Smith ordered his men out of the fort. He commissioned George Percy and John Martin to set up a fort nearer to the south on the Nansemond River; and Smith commissioned Francis West (son of Thomas West, Baron De La Warr) to establish a fort nearer to Powhatan town. Smith hoped this would relieve the constant sickness and food shortages, and separate him from the ranking gentlemen. Percy and West could directly trade with the Nansemond and Powhatans letting Smith maintain a storehouse in Jamestown.

Fortunately, this did reduce the stress in the fort and enabled many settlers to recover from disease. Unfortunately, this plan ended in disaster. Percy and Martin took 100 men and camped adjacent to the Nansemond town. Once in place, they attempted to open negotiations with the weroance. The two messengers sent to speak with the chief never returned. Percy found a Nansemond man rowing the next day and asked him why his messengers did not return. The man told Percy that the messengers were sacrificed, and their brains were scraped out with mussel shells. The Nansemond chief, Wyhohomo, assumed the armed camp planned harm on his town. Percy and Martin decided to punish the tribe for killing their messengers. Since the first landing, misunderstandings had led to occasional killings on both sides, many mistakes had been adjudicated by Chief Powhatan and John Smith, but now, out on their own, Martin and Percy decided to torch the Nansemond village. Percy writes in his *Trewe Relation* how Martin came ashore to join the encampment and "we beat the savages out of their Island burned their houses ransacked their temples, took down the corpses of their dead kings from of their tombs and carried away their pearls, copper, and bracelets where with they do decorate their kings funerals."

Percy understood what he and Martin had done. They desecrated a Powhatan temple and stole the funeral finery of deceased chiefs. This action was unforgivable. Powhatan leadership transitioned from the peace chief to the war chief. Chief Opechancanough alerted his other war chiefs and prepared to challenge the English.

Percy's past of failed endeavors raised its head again at the little fort built outside the Nansemond town. Percy departed to go tell John Smith about the destruction of the town and left the 100 men in the small earthen fort they had begun building. The Nansemond besieged the remaining men and slowly picked them off until 50 were able to escape a few weeks later. Percy abandoned his company and failed to return with reinforcements.

Simultaneously, Francis West, with 140 men, went to Powhatan town intending to build a palisaded fort near the future site of Richmond. Chief Powhatan's son, Parahunt, acted as the weroance of the town and came out several times to speak with West. West offered to buy the town. Chief Parahunt refused further negotiation unless John Smith came. Smith did come, bringing his guard of the "good shottes" prepared for trouble. Smith and West agreed to give one piece of copper to each household who paid a yearly tribute of one bushel of corn and to protect the Powhatans from the Monacans to the west. For unknown reasons Parahunt agreed to this. Parahunt's definition of "sold" only turned over authority, leaving his tribe in their homes. Smith notes the "Salvage Fort, readie built, and prettily fortified with poles and barkes of trees." The town included many "dry houses for lodgings and neere two hundred accres of ground ready to be planted." The English named the fort "Nonsuch."

This arrangement soured quickly. Smith and his guard returned to Jamestown leaving West and his men in Nonsuch. West's men showed their colors as rough adventurers, daily abusing their neighbors. During three months of misuse the Powhatan people began striking back. Whenever Englishmen left the town, they were ambushed: 50 men disappeared in this manner. West's garrison of 140 dropped to 90, retreating to Jamestown in late October 1609. The purchased town reverted to Parahunt's control.

John Smith's clever idea to get men out of the fort bought him time but instigated two conflicts. One on the south end of the James River where Percy and West desecrated the Nansemond homes and temple. And another in the north at Chief Powhatan's birth town where the English "purchased" and abandoned the fortified town.

While returning downriver after the purchase of Powhatan town, John Smith, "accidentallie ... fired his powder-bag, which tore the flesh from his body and thighes, nine or ten inches square in a most pittifull manner; but to quench the tormenting fire, frying him in his cloaths he leaped over-boord into the deepe river." John Smith's leadership ended abruptly. Needing a surgeon to repair the extreme burns on his abdomen, Smith lay in agony in Jamestown until he departed for England in October 1609. In Smith's *Generall Historie* he records his departure, attempting to paint a positive outlook for the colony after his two and a half years of work. He stated they were left with:

> three ships, seaven boats, commodities readie to trade, the harvest newly gathered, ten weeks provision in the store, foure hundred nintie and od[d] persons, twentie-foure Peeces of Ordnance, three hundred Muskets, Snaphances, and Firelockes, Shot, Powder, and Match sufficient, Curats, Pikes, Swords, and Morrios, more then men; the Salvages, their language, and habitations well knowne to an hundred well trayned and expert Souldiers; Nets for fishing; Tooles of all sorts to worke; apparell to supply our wants; six Mares and a Horse; five or six hundred Swine; as many Hennes and Chickens; some Goats; some sheep.

For the rest of his life Smith blamed the gentlemen for squandering what he had left them. Smith's list depicts a well-armed and well-fed populace. Smith had no idea what the future held for those left behind in Jamestown in winter 1609. The presidency of Jamestown fell to George Percy. The first blows of a full-scale war were struck. The best leader, negotiator, and sole trusted agent of several tribes had left the colony.

Within a week of Smith's departure, Opechancanough put the confederacy into full revolt against the English. Raids at every English outpost forced Percy to withdraw into the Jamestown Fort. With more men back in the fort, the food stores dwindled quickly. Percy sent John Ratcliffe to build a fort at Point Comfort to develop a fishery and to look out for any relief vessels entering the Chesapeake. The fort was dubbed Fort Algernon and became the best decision of Percy's presidency. Returning from Point Comfort, Ratcliffe and Percy received an invitation from Chief Powhatan; a messenger brought gifts of venison and promised peace to the Englishmen if they came to Opechancanough's village of Pamunkey to trade weapons for food. Percy eagerly accepted this invitation, sending Ratcliffe and 100 men to the village bearing weapons for trade in November 1609.

Ratcliffe marched his company of 100 men out of the Jamestown Fort, marching some on the shore and sailing some in the pinnace as he approached the Pamunkey town. Opechancanough waited for many soldiers to enter the town and begin collecting bushels of wheat and corn. As the men carried baskets toward the pinnace, the Pamunkey warriors attacked. Warriors took Ratcliffe prisoner and began a ritual sacrifice of him. Thirty-three English soldiers plus John Ratcliffe died in the village. Warriors streamed out of the fort and attempted to seize the pinnace. The Englishmen fought off the warriors and retreated to Jamestown. Later Thomas Savage, an Englishman living among the Pamunkeys, confirmed that Ratcliffe was ritualistically executed, cut limb from limb with his skin and head removed last. This horrific death put great fear into the hungry survivors at Jamestown.

After the Ratcliffe fiasco, Francis West betrayed President Percy. Percy begged West to sail out to trade with the Patawomecks, who remained friendly despite the Powhatan war footing. West took 36 soldiers and the small vessel the *Swallow*. The Patawomecks often acted independently and traded corn to the English. Once the vessel was loaded, the soldiers suddenly drew their swords and cut off the heads of the attending Patawomecks. The townspeople fled as the Englishmen boarded their vessel and sailed east, away from Percy and Jamestown. West's unannounced departure took much-needed food supplies and destroyed the last friendly relationship the Englishmen had among the independent tribes.

Percy's options ran low as he wrote, "[West] left us in that extreme misery and want. Now all of us at Jamestown began to feel the sharp prick of hunger." Powhatan warriors then assembled the largest force yet

This painting by Sydney King depicts Jamestown in a peaceful moment, but the narrow strip leading to the fort can clearly be seen. (MPI/ Getty Images)

seen by the English. As many as 800 warriors breached the guard shack on the spit of land connecting Jamestown to the mainland and surrounded the fort just outside musket range. Percy and 320 settlers were cut off from trade, foraging, and communication with Fort Algernon to the south. A small garrison of perhaps 30 men thrived at Fort Algernon during the winter of 1609. The 320 trapped inside Jamestown Fort dwindled from starvation and disease. Extreme conditions saw settlers consuming anything edible within the fort. Desperate for food, some ventured outside, but any party that left the walls of the fort and neared the forest received a volley of arrows or disappeared into the brush never to return.

1610, DELIVERANCE AND THE FIRST OFFENSIVE

The six-month siege of Jamestown continued until May 1610. Powhatan warriors departed the island to plant their own fields of corn, beans, and wheat. Percy finally could send word to Fort Algernon asking for help. Of the 320 in Jamestown in November, only 60 survived by May 1610. Percy began at once shipping survivors to Fort Algernon, hoping to separate the healthy from the diseased. Luckily for Percy, help arrived. Thomas Gates and George Somers survived the crash landing of the *Sea Venture* on Bermuda in July of 1609. Spending the year constructing two new ships from the wreckage, Thomas Gates arrived on May 21, 1610, to find the colony suffering and destitute.

Gates and Somers spent a week discussing with Percy the best way to save the colony. The fate of the English Empire, the pride of English adventurers, the blood of the many deceased, and the immense amount of money spent on the colony caused Gates and Percy to clash over how to proceed. Percy and Martin eventually convinced Gates to abandon the fort. Some men wanted to burn it to the ground, but Gates prevented them. Four ships formed up to sail for Newfoundland. The 90 survivors of the starving time and the 150 who survived the Bermuda ordeal all abandoned Jamestown. Departing on June 7, 1610, the four vessels anchored off Point Comfort to load the last of the supplies from Fort Algernon.

For 72 hours, no Englishmen stood on Powhatan soil. Chief Powhatan and Opechancanough would have found the collapsed walls of Jamestown a symbol of their victory. Opechancanough's methods of constant ambush and abduction had driven the English into the sea as hoped. An unanswerable historical question is why did the Powhatans not burn or occupy the fort at Jamestown? In the 1580s, the Ajácan Mission was torn down stone by stone leaving no trace of the Spanish in the Chesapeake. If Jamestown had been dismantled on June 8 and 9, would the English have given up? If Powhatans had dug up the recently buried cannons and muskets and used European arms against returning Europeans, would the English have been able to assault the fort? The Powhatans apparently left the abandoned fort alone.

On the morning of June 8, 1610, the refugees of Jamestown awaited the tide to take them out to sea. On the horizon two vessels approached and a lone longboat rowed into view of the awaiting vessels. The men on board called to Gates and Percy, announcing the arrival of Thomas West, Baron of De La Warr, the newly appointed governor of Virginia. The arrival of

De La Warr's fleet on the exact day that Gates and Percy tried to retreat from Jamestown owed much of its luck to Samuel Argall. The young captain, who developed a faster route to Virginia, led De La Warr's fleet to Jamestown in just nine weeks, arriving literally moments before Jamestown became a second lost colony.

Argall miraculously navigated De La Warr's fleet to arrive just in time to catch Percy and Gates' abandonment of Jamestown, preventing another lost colony. Artwork by Sydney King for the National Park Service. (MPI/Getty Images)

Baron De La Warr, Thomas West, received his commission from the Virginia Company to act as governor-for-life in Virginia. De La Warr brought a lifetime of political connections and a talent for sound administration to the faltering colony. Ordering the refugees back to Jamestown caused heartache to the emaciated survivors from 1609. The complaints caused De La Warr to abandon civil governance and convert the colony to martial rule. This is referred to as the establishment of *The Lawes Divine, Morall and Martiall*, which would remain in effect in Virginia until 1619. With this, De La Warr instituted a new chain of command, appointing Gates as the lieutenant governor, Percy as esquire, and Argall, Yeardley, and Martin as company commanders of 50 men.

English Chain of Command during the First Anglo-Powhatan War

Name	Role
Sir Thomas West, Baron De La Warr	Lord Governor and Captain-General; supreme commander
Sir Thomas Gates	Lieutenant Governor
Sir Thomas Dale	Marshal of Virginia
Sir George Somers	Admiral of Virginia; Captain of *Sea Venture* and *Patience*
Capt. Christopher Newport	Vice-Admiral of Virginia
Capt. George Percy	Commander of James Fort
Capt. Edward Brewster	Commander, De La Warr's company
Capt. George Yeardley	Commander, Gates' company
Sir Ferdinando Wainman	Master of Ordnance, General of Horse
Capt. Thomas Holecroft	Commander of a 50-man company
Capt. Samuel Argall	Commander of a 50-man company; Captain of *Discovery* and *Treasure*
Capt. Thomas Lawson	Commander of a 50-man company
Capt. John Martin	Master of the Battery Works for Iron
Capt. George Webb	Sergeant-Major of James Fort
Master Daniel Tucker	Clerk of the Store
Master Robert Wilde	Clerk of the Store
William Strachey, Esq.	Colony Secretary and Council Recorder
Master Ralph Hamor	Clerk of the Council
Master Browne	Clerk of the Council

The colony's 50-man companies acted as separate forces to raid nearby. (J. Frederick Fausz, "An 'Abundance of Blood Shed on Both Sides': England's First Indian War, 1609–1614," *The Virginia Magazine of History and Biography*, vol. 98, no. 1 (January 1, 1990))

De La Warr ignored Percy's warnings about the danger the Powhatans held for them. Gates, despite supporting Percy, could not say first hand that he had seen atrocities by the indigenous population. De La Warr sent emissaries to Powhatan to negotiate peace. Powhatan rejected the emissaries replying that he did not believe De La Warr was as great a chief as he claimed because Powhatan knew that great men in England traveled by carriage. Powhatan said if De La Warr came to his town of Orapax in a carriage he would speak with him. After the negotiations, an Englishman attempting to fish was carried by the wind to the opposite shore of the James River. As soon as the man drew close to the shore a party of Powhatans emerged from the woods, captured, and sacrificed the man there on the beach in full view of Jamestown. Stunned, Gates and De La Warr willingly prepared an offensive to prevent further Powhatan attacks.

De La Warr and Thomas Gates prepared the first planned English offensive in the New World. After discussion with Percy, De La Warr and Gates sought food and cropland. To achieve this goal De La Warr planned to use the English sailing advantages to strike suddenly along the rivers. On July 9, 1610, the first column departed Jamestown. Gates led the company, primarily of musketeers, to Fort Algernon where they marched on the village of Kecoughtan. Kecoughtan had not been a part of the starving time siege and had traded with the detachment at Fort Algernon throughout the year. The Kecoughtans had received no indication that the English had chosen their village to start their offensive. As the musketeers approached the village, the sounds of their drummers drew the villagers out. In Powhatan culture, a parade of music and men represented a festival or religious event. Seeing the townspeople gathered in the open, Gates ordered his men to fire. The veterans of Dutch wars, formed in textbook lines and files, accompanied by drummers, executed their drills firing into the crowd. No battle ensued but the killing of many Kecoughtans destroyed the only friendly tribe left near Jamestown. The remaining villagers fled, abandoning the town. Gates returned to De La Warr announcing the region around Fort Algernon as cleared and was available for farming. De La Warr commissioned several officers to go to Kecoughtan and build two forts to enable the creation of a homestead to support Fort Algernon; the homestead eventually became known as the city of Hampton.

This first English conquest generated a counterattack just five days later. On July 16, the blockhouse which defended the narrow strip of land connecting Jamestown Island to the mainland had 20 men defending it. The blockhouse was a traditional English-style blockhouse likely 10 feet by 10 feet on the first floor with a 12-foot by 12-foot second floor creating an elevated firing position with a wooden roof.

Several Paspahegh warriors charged down the spit of land killing four defenders before the rest loaded their muskets to repulse them. Paspahegh town became the next target. De La Warr appointed Percy, the next highest-ranking gentleman, to lead the attack on the Paspahegh, but knowing his lack of martial success, Captains John Davis and William West acted as his lieutenants. Percy wrote:

I departed from Jamestown the 9th of August 1610 and the same night landed within three miles of Paspahegh town. Then drawing my soldiers into battle line placing a captain or Lieutenant at every file, we marched towards the town... I commanded every leader to draw away his file before me to beset the savages houses that none might escape.

Spreading out, Percy instructed Davis and West to wait for the signal to attack all at once. Shooting a pistol into the air signaled all 70 Englishmen to attack. "We fell in upon them putting some 15 or 16 to the sword and the rest to flight." The Paspahegh chief Wowinchopunk had resisted the English since their first arrival, having led the attack on May 26, 1607. The men of Jamestown had three years of grudges to unleash on the chief and his town. The attackers ransacked the homes taking as much food as they could carry and captured Wowinchopunk's wife and sons, executing all three before the end of the day.

Built in 1750, Fort Edward in Nova Scotia has the oldest original blockhouse in North America. The Jamestown blockhouse matched this style. (Hantsheroes/ Wikimedia Commons)

The next week saw two more raids, one by Captain Davis and one by Captain Edward Brewster. Both used their full company of 50 musketeers. Davis marched overland to the Chickahominy village where his men formed up and watched the town flee. He then burned the village and again captured as much corn as his men could carry. Brewster sailed south to attack the village of Warraskoyack. Newly arrived with De La Warr, Brewster hoped to avenge his brother who had been killed in 1607. Brewster brought 100 soldiers with him; his arrival caused the tribe to flee, allowing Brewster, unopposed, to desecrate their temple and torch the whole village. His men then harvested the Warraskoyack's corn and returned to Jamestown.

The first phase of De La Warr's strategy was complete. All tribes downriver from Jamestown, Kecoughtan, Warraskoyack, and Nansemond, were reduced to ashes and their corn horded within the Jamestown settlement. The nearest upriver tribes of Paspahegh and Chickahominy were crippled. This modeled similar strategies pursued in Ireland. As Alison Games writes in *The Web of Empire*, "the English learned to assume the mantle of conquerors" in Ireland. This same mantle seemed to have arrived with De La Warr in Virginia.

De La Warr then began phase two, find gold and iron. He still shied away from the plantation model, wanting to exploit the land as originally planned by the company. The now well-supplied settlement deployed a 200-man expedition in a barque, a three-masted square-rigged vessel, up the James River to reoccupy the area abandoned by Thomas West in the fall of 1609. Recorded in Percy's *Trewe Relation*, the subsequent events are transcribed into modern English:

My Lord intended to search for minerals and to make further proof of the iron mines. He sent many men in a barque up to the falls of the James going past the Appomattox village. The barque rested to refill their water supply. [15 men went ashore to fill their water barrels.] Indian women emerged and enticed the men up to their houses, offering them a feast. Our men forgetting the wiles of the savages, like greedy fools accepted. They held food in higher esteem than their own lives and safety. For when the Indians had them in their houses, they found a fitting time, when the men least feared danger and the Indians fell upon them and slew many and wounded the rest.

First Anglo-Powhatan War: Events of 1610–14

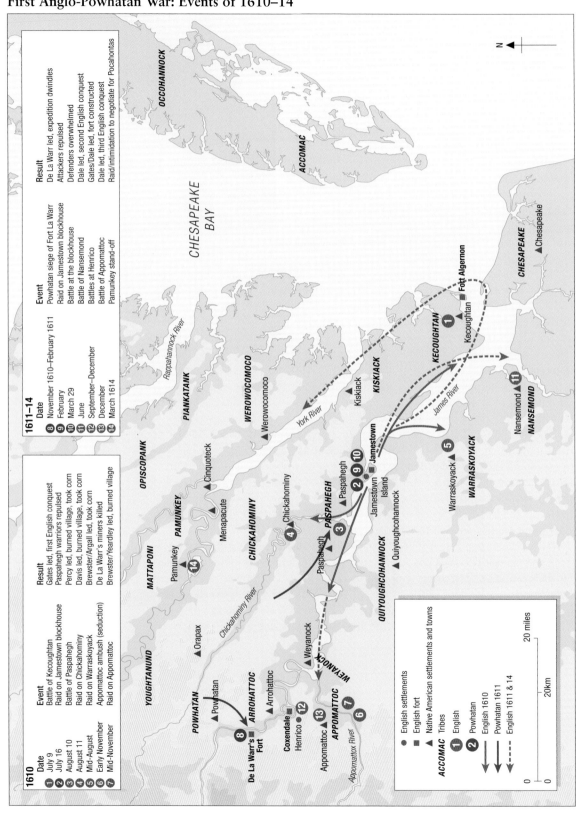

With his men enticed by women, De La Warr's expedition had suffered 15 deaths before arrival at Henrico. In Percy's writing, his frustration at the men falling into the trap comes through. The officers of Jamestown still acted autonomously despite De La Warr's heavy-handedness. De La Warr commissioned Brewster and Yeardley to avenge the killings at Appomattoc. Brewster's men traveled to the town and fired volleys into the town, killing many of the Appomattoc warriors and wounding the queen with musket fire. De La Warr personally traveled upriver to establish Fort La Warr. This fort remained near the Powhatan town site and immediately received harassing attacks from Powhatan bowmen.

Determined to stay at the site, De La Warr and his nephew William West kept 200 men with them at the newly constructed fort. As winter set in, the nearby Powhatans once again began a winter siege of the fort. Like the experience of those trapped in Jamestown the previous winter, any Englishman who ventured outside of Fort La Warr was ambushed. De La Warr attempted to sally out of the fort several times but each time was repulsed and driven back into the fort. The Powhatans started calling out taunts to the trapped men, goading them about the high number of swords and muskets they had stolen from dead bodies. From December 1610 to March 1611, De La Warr's health declined. Finally, in March, he and his men were able to escape the fort, sailing back to Jamestown.

1611, THE AGE OF DALE

De La Warr departed the colony quickly; he confessed that in his current state of health he was incapable of governing the colony. On March 28, De La Warr commissioned George Percy to act as governor once again until reinforcements arrived. De La Warr, Gates, and a contingent of 70 men departed Jamestown. Smith's departure in October of 1609 had spurred full retaliation on all fronts against the English. With De La Warr's departure, a massive Powhatan force stormed Jamestown Island. Chief Opechancanough wisely followed the comings and goings of the English leaders. The full-scale raid on the blockhouse occurred the very next day after De La Warr's departure; 300 warriors lay in wait to attack by the evening of March 29.

A small detachment of Paspahegh warriors slowly approached the blockhouse, guarding the narrow causeway which led to Jamestown. A Lieutenant Pullock was the officer in charge of 20 soldiers meant to defend the blockhouse. Percy writes in his *Trewe Relation* that Lieutenant Pullock, "showing more valor than wit, more fury than judgement," exited the blockhouse with all 20 men to chase the small party back into the woods. 300 warriors appeared in the brush and "let fly their arrows as thick as hail … and cut them all down in a moment, the arrows which they had shot being so many in number that the ground there abouts was almost covered with them." George Percy then sent Lieutenant Abbot with 50 musketeers to drive them away. Not knowing what had befallen Pullock, Abbot's men approached and heard the warriors cheering and chanting "Paspahegh." From a ranged position, Abbott fired volleys and dispersed the massed warriors. Muskets began to prove their worth defensively and offensively as more military veterans wielded them on the fields of Virginia. Chief Opechancanough did not have the strength to eliminate the fort, and it was the wrong season to begin a siege.

Percy conservatively recalled English forces back into Jamestown until reinforcements and a new governor arrived. Fort Algernon was abandoned when De La Warr took the 200 men north to search for gold, leaving Jamestown once again as the only occupied English settlement. Opechancanough again laid a siege, preventing the Englishmen from venturing out. This time the fort was well provisioned, well garrisoned, and able to comfortably wait for the situation to change. Ironically, Percy found himself in a similar position to that of 1610. In May of 1610 Thomas Gates appeared just in time to save the survivors. Now, in May 1611, Thomas Dale arrived to relieve Percy from the burden of command.

Thomas Dale brought much-needed leadership experience and energy to the colony. Percy, never having been an inspiring leader, remained content to relax inside the fort while warriors prowled the edges of the island. Accompanying Dale was Thomas Gates, returning from England after escorting De La Warr home. Together Dale and Gates developed the next phase of the First Anglo-Powhatan War. Thus far, the Englishmen had secured a significant amount of food supplies to stave off starvation for the rest of the year and they had cleared the downriver lands of enemy combatants. Thanks to De La Warr's experience in Virginia, he ensured that Dale and Gates came prepared; marching ashore with Dale came 300 veterans from the Dutch Wars for Independence. This large body of men doubled the population of Jamestown and enabled Dale to prepare a thorough campaign plan. The three companies were well trained in modern military tactics and set to training the rest of the garrison who had grown idle "neither fighting nor farming." Dale reinstituted the martial law established by De La Warr. Dale unashamedly executed or punished any who questioned his authority. Much later Dale's government received accusations of making slaves of Englishmen in Virginia, but given the poor leadership and judgment demonstrated by Percy and other previous gentlemen of the colony, Dale's draconian style seemed necessary to build an ordered society out of adventurers. Historian J. Frederick Fausz sees Dale's government addressing "crucial concerns for order and survival in a combat zone of a distant war with no precedents." The extreme punishments meted out by Dale enabled the colony to organize; any absconders were harshly executed.

This draconian rule had the secondhand effect of harsh and brutal treatment of all indigenous peoples. Under Dale's reign, English patrols who encountered Powhatans often killed them on the spot instead of capturing or trading. Some historians question if this harsh lifestyle began a cycle of English dominance in the New World. As Fausz postulates, "The most haunting implication of this tragic first war is that there were probably reluctant warriors on both sides, with more in common than three centuries of racist rhetoric permit us to appreciate, who were goaded into mutual slaughter." The violence continued as the Anglo-Powhatan War entered its third summer. Chief Powhatan still had not been seen since his withdrawal in 1609. Opechancanough seemed to continue his generalship of the Powhatan peoples.

Thomas Dale, veteran of the Low Countries and Ireland, examined the colonial maps and heard the

Dale's veterans each brought the latest armor and weaponry from Europe. A helmet, plates, and tassets like these could have been worn by such men. (Rogers Fund, The Metropolitan Museum of Art, 1919)

accounts from Percy of what had occurred over the last three campaign seasons. Dale instituted a new plan to trap Chief Powhatan to bring about a quick surrender. Where the first offensive in 1610 captured farmlands and food, Dale hoped to squeeze Powhatan lands up against enemies from all sides. Dale understood the Powhatans feared the Monacans and the Massawomacks and hoped to create a choice for Powhatan: migrate and face war with his generational foes or be harried and trapped by the English. To begin this plan Dale needed to clear the south of enemies. The Kecoughtans and Warraskoyacks capitulated but the Nansemonds remained stalwart on their own inlet and river. If the Nansemonds could be cleared, Dale and Jamestown would control from the mouth of the James to the Chickahominy River.

Dale prepared his company of 100 men to depart for the Nansemond tribe. The Nansemonds had four villages: Mattanock, Nansemond, Mantoughquemed, and Teracosick. The weroance resided in the village of Nansemond. The Englishmen sailed from Jamestown to land on the doorstep of the Nansemond tribal region. The flat terrain made for many good landing sites. Disembarking from the vessels, Dale's men were fully armored. Given that Smith claimed there were "Marions more than men" as of 1609 the likely armor worn by Dale's men were morin helmets. The body army comprised a chest and backplate. This can be assumed from the injuries received by the three captains present in the battle. "Francis West was shot in the thigh and Captain Martin in the arm. Thomas Dale himself narrowly escaped for an arrow light just upon the edge of his head piece." Percy goes on to write that Dale had "diverse encounters and skirmished with the savages both by land and water." This implies that the Nansemonds harried them while still on boats. Dale likely had to clear landing sites with musket fire.

Previous encounters had seen Native Americans withdraw when musket formation had sufficient stand-off distance. Since there were several encounters, this points to the idea that Dale relied on more of a mixed formation of pike and shot. Dale's men in head and body armor endured the firing of many arrows. The formations of the Nansemonds, confused by the ineffectiveness of their arrows, brought out "conjurers and priests" who began making incantations to bring rain to extinguish the musketeers' powder. Percy reported "conjured" fire balls and chants over the heads of the Nansemond warriors. Dale's 100 men prevailed; fighting for two days across several fields they pushed the Nansemonds away, burned their towns, and cut down their corn. Percy noted the last time the Nansemonds fought the English, Percy and Martin's companies had been torn up by arrow volleys. The stunning realization that the arrows were ineffective challenged the Nansemonds' world view of archery as a form of spiritual power. The morale of the Powhatans weakened with each English victory.

With the Nansemonds conquered south and downriver of Jamestown, Dale turned north and upriver. The long-time goal of creating a settlement near the falls of the James River prompted Dale to plan the third expedition to the north. In 1609, Francis West lost a whole company, 50 men, after "purchasing" Powhatan town. In late 1610, De La Warr brought two companies north, constructing Fort La Warr near the falls of the James River. Constant skirmishes and harassments trapped De La Warr in his fort for months until he too retreated to Jamestown. Now in the fall of 1611 Dale prepared his attempt to establish a fort at the falls of the James River.

Dale's attack at Nansemond, 1611 (PP. 66–67)

The Nansemond people lived in several villages along the Nansemond River (**1**). Villages contained living, religious, storage, and meeting spaces. Warfare between the Powhatan Confederacy and their neighbors rarely involved the targeting of structures, yet the wars against the English normalized the destruction of storage spaces and dwellings during raids.

Powhatan Confederacy warriors of all tribes relied heavily on bows as their primary weapon in combat. Crescent moon-shaped formations massed arrow volleys and were followed by surging attacks of clubmen to dispatch the wounded (**2**). War chiefs led the formations and often coordinated warriors from several tribes. The cloak depicted on the weroance (**3**) matches the cloak worn

by Chief Powhatan. Shamans (**4**) of Nansemond joined the last day of battle against the English force and attempted to conjure spells and rain dances to halt the English muskets.

Thomas Dale brought experienced veterans, each fully dressed in the latest Dutch infantry armor. A debate remains on whether Dale's three 100-man companies assumed the standard Dutch formation of musket-pike-musket (**5**) during the Powhatan War or if they followed the *Lawes Divine* encouraging non-musketeers to take up the sword and buckler. Given the flat and marshy terrain of Nansemond and the threat of surging clubman attacks, this illustration interprets English warriors using 10-foot short pikes, a likely tool which also took influence from veterans' experience in the Low Country.

In August, a supply fleet arrived delivering 250 additional veteran soldiers, raising the English population to 750. The crowded sickly settlements of Jamestown and Point Comfort encouraged Dale to quickly establish a third zone. Dale ordered Captain Edward Brewster to march 200 men overland to the narrow island-like peninsula later known as Ferrar Island. Dale sailed upriver with an additional 100 men to form a garrison of 300 on the island. During the march and clearing of land, Powhatan warriors constantly harassed and harried the English. Brewster reported "diverse assaults and encounters" along the several days' march.

Historic woodcut of a musketeer and pikeman at the turn of the 17th century. (mikroman6/Getty Images)

As the new walls of the fort were cut, dug, and planted, reckless Powhatan warriors (led by a radical war chief named Nemattanew) sprinted into the English camp to shoot arrows into tents and doorways of the mid-construction structures. Thomas Dale stoically maintained order, repulsing these daily attacks until the fort was complete. They named it Fort Henry and began clearing land to the west to prepare farmlands for the coming spring. Despite this major success personally led by Dale, his draconian hand drove many men to desert and join the Powhatan tribe only a few miles distant. Dale ordered several deserters recaptured, upon which he executed them by being "broken up upon a wheel."

Thomas Gates managed Jamestown and Point Comfort, while Dale focused on Fort Henry and its newly built homesteads surrounding the fort. Late in the winter of 1611, Dale led a raid on the Appomattoc tribes; no warriors opposed the operation. Three years of prolonged war had drained the Powhatan warriors to the point of dismay. Powhatans had not won an engagement since the blockhouse attack in March, and any Englishmen killed in ambush or battle were replaced by fresh fully armored troops in the next wave of supply ships. As the year 1612 began, the organized violence in the First Anglo-Powhatan War ended.

1612, 1613, AND 1614 TUG OF WAR

Thomas Dale, Thomas Gates, and George Percy divided the administration of the now sturdy colony. Three major strongpoints guarded the water access for the James River: Fort Algernon, Jamestown Fort (which had grown to a five-sided fort with three bulwarks), and Fort Henry. A balance of power brought a calm from the violence of the previous years. From 1609 to 1610 the Powhatans felt they had the ability to drive the English into the sea or at least into submission. De La Warr and Dale's well-executed campaigns in 1610 and 1611 put Jamestown on a footing able to stand toe to toe with the Powhatan Confederacy. This balance of power led English men and Powhatan Weroances to look for new avenues toward peace. Far away in London the reports of Dale's harsh methods and the continued loss of life to sickness caused the Virginia Company to stop sending more warriors to America. The Powhatans had no way of knowing that the seemingly endless supply of armored warriors stopped in 1612. The Virginia Company told De La Warr, still the true governor despite his absence, that the colony needed to become profitable. De La Warr sent his favored sea captain, Samuel Argall, once again to Virginia.

Argall, like Christopher Newport before him, arrived in Virginia not fully aware of the trials and tribulations faced by the colonists. Argall knew many battles raged along the Virginia Peninsula, but he also knew there were many more tribes than those surrounding Jamestown. Argall on repeat voyages to Virginia reopened trade with tribes on the eastern shore and tribes to the north. He found several tribes eager to trade for European goods and make peace with Jamestown. To the north Argall reacquainted himself with Chief Japssus whom he had traded with back in 1609. On a return trading venture Japssus told Argall that Powhatan's favored daughter, Pocahontas, was a visitor in his town. Argall bribed Japssus into assisting in her capture. Japssus met with the other weroances of the Patawomeck, and they decided that they would break their alliance with Powhatan and realign with the English. The tug of war for Virginia began to change. Japssus and his queen invited Pocahontas to dine with Captain Argall on board Argall's ship *The Treasure*. Upon boarding, Argall took her prisoner and transported her to Jamestown.

Dale and Argall at once reached out to negotiate with Chief Powhatan. They hoped to ransom Pocahontas for a peace treaty. Powhatan never responded. Confused by the silence from the formerly verbose and inviting Mamanatowick, Dale and Argall bargained separately with tribes on the eastern shore and the nearby rivers. The Patawomeck, the Accomac, and the Chickahominy abandoned Powhatan to ally with the English. During the years 1612 to 1614, Argall's regular and predictable arrivals for trade and his obedience to Dale's hierarchy created a stable community the Powhatan tribes understood and respected. Pocahontas remained in Jamestown for a year and a half. She had previously visited many times in 1608 and 1609; the men of Jamestown were pleased to meet her again. One man, John Rolfe, fell in love with her. That is not a Disney fantasy; John Rolfe left many diaries and letters behind. In many of his writings he agonized over the cultural difference and chided himself for loving a "savage." He wrote to priests and mentors in England asking for their advice. His mentors replied that if she converted to Christianity, he should be proud to take part in the assimilation and Christianization of the Powhatans. John Rolfe then asked Dale's permission to marry Pocahontas.

Dale took this opportunity to definitively finish the war against the Powhatans. In March 1614, Dale sailed up the York River and landed several companies on the banks of the Pamunkey town Matchot. War chief Opechancanough was the "king" of the Pamunkey. Dale knew the Pamunkey warriors represented the backbone of Powhatan's armies. If the Pamunkey could be defeated or agree to peace Dale believed the war could be ended. Dale anchored offshore from the Pamunkey towns and sent emissaries to request audience with Chief Powhatan. The reply came that Powhatan was three days away, but Chief Opechancanough could speak with him in his place. Dale refused. Dale and his men waited for three days then began burning homes on the edge of the water. This sabotage brought emissaries back to Dale. Finally, the communication made it through translation that the Englishman wished to marry Pocahontas and end the war. Brothers of Pocahontas came out to meet with John Rolfe and meet with Pocahontas privately. They believed their sister's wish was genuine, because the brothers reported to Dale that Powhatan agreed to the marriage. The large force of men and ships returned downriver to Jamestown with Pocahontas. Dale wrote a long and detailed letter back to London reporting that the war was settled. The Virginia Company investors who had previously threatened to stop funding the colony due to lack of profits needed to hear the war was over and business could resume. With the declaration of the war over and a marriage pact to seal the peace, London planners and Powhatan chiefs viewed the war as complete.

This woodcut from 1619 depicts Pocahontas' brother conversing with her during the stand-off at Matchot. (Courtesy of the John Carter Brown Library)

The story of Rolfe and Pocahontas is told in many places; the significance in this narrative is mutual respect and understanding of the marriage pact by both cultures. The Powhatans and the English shared the cultural event of marriages for alliances. The 1614 marriage of Rolfe and Pocahontas restored the personal alliance that had collapsed with John Smith in late 1609. Powhatan invited John Smith into his confederacy and granted him status and lands as weroance of Jamestown. Smith overstepped his role by alienating the nearby tribes and forcing other weroances to obey him, even directly threatening Chief Powhatan and Opechancanough. Upon Smith's departure in 1609, no other Englishman had a personal relationship with Chief Powhatan. Rolfe's marriage restored a personal relationship amid the English settlements. Powhatan recognized Rolfe as a subordinate of Dale. Rolfe and Pocahontas created the personal relationship Chief Powhatan wanted to allow them back into his confederacy. Even if the English did not see it that way, the Powhatan Mamanatowick and weroances once again could recognize the English as an equal player among the tribes of the confederacy.

THE CAMPAIGN OF THE SECOND ANGLO-POWHATAN WAR

Relative peace reigned in Virginia from 1612 to 1622. This decade saw exponential growth for the English. Disease struck the Native American population of Virginia as more Europeans landed in the Chesapeake, weakening Powhatan tribes as the English population grew. Chief Opitchapam became Mamanatowick with the death of Chief Powhatan in 1618. English settlements and plantations sprung up along the James River between the controlled English zones and some even beyond Jamestown's reach.

Governor George Yeardley brought the Great Charter to Virginia in 1619, fundamentally changing the way land and laborers operated in the colony. Secretary of the colony George Sandys helped transport 3,500 new colonists to Virginia between 1619 and 1622. Along with this influx of settlers came a decree to intentionally convert the Powhatans to Christianity. George Thorpe arrived as the deputy of a new Indian College to convert and train Powhatans. Thorpe had a genuine desire to help the Powhatans having adopted a Powhatan child brought to England by John Rolfe in 1615. Thorpe

The growth of English control, 1614–22

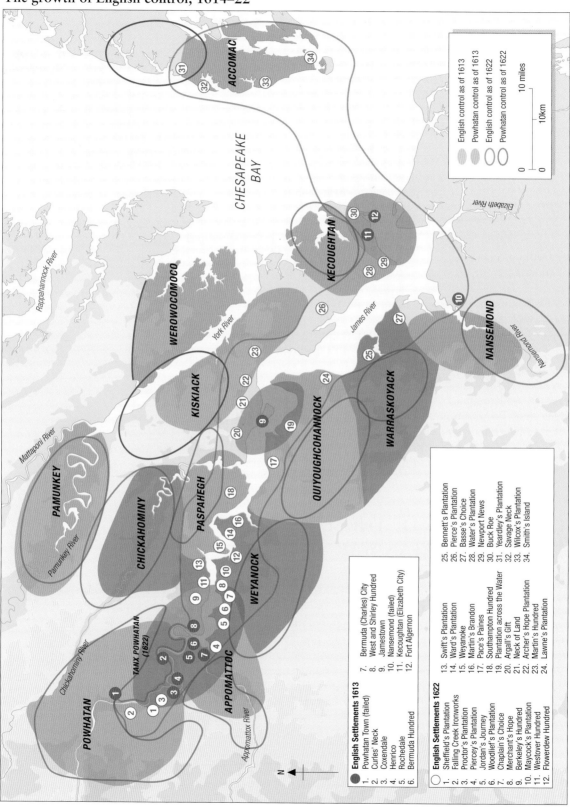

CHESAPEAKE BAY

ACCOMAC

Rappahannock River

Elizabeth River

WEROWOCOMOCO

KECOUGHTAN

York River

James River

NANSEMOND

Nansemond River

Mattaponi River

KISKIACK

PAMUNKEY

Pamunkey River

CHICKAHOMINY

PASPAHEGH

QUIYOUGHCOHANNOCK

WARRASKOYACK

WEYANOCK

TANX POWHATAN (1622)

APPOMATTOC

POWHATAN

Chickahominy River

Appomattox River

N

English control as of 1613
Powhatan control as of 1613
English control as of 1622
Powhatan control as of 1622

0   10 miles
0   10km

English Settlements 1613
1. Powhatan Town (failed)
2. Curles' Neck
3. Coxendale
4. Henrico
5. Rochedale
6. Bermuda Hundred
7. Bermuda (Charles) City
8. West and Shirley Hundred
9. Jamestown
10. Nansemond (failed)
11. Kecoughtan (Elizabeth City)
12. Fort Algernon

English Settlements 1622
1. Sheffield's Plantation
2. Falling Creek Ironworks
3. Proctor's Plantation
4. Piercey's Plantation
5. Jordan's Journey
6. Woodlief's Plantation
7. Chaplain's Choice
8. Merchant's Hope
9. Berkeley's Hundred
10. Maycock's Plantation
11. Westover Hundred
12. Flowerdew Hundred
13. Swift's Plantation
14. Ward's Plantation
15. Weyanoke
16. Martin's Brandon
17. Pace's Paines
18. Southampton Hundred
19. Plantation across the Water
20. Argall's Gift
21. Neck of Land
22. Archer's Hope Plantation
23. Martin's Hundred
24. Lawne's Plantation
25. Bennett's Plantation
26. Pierce's Plantation
27. Basse's Choice
28. Water's Plantation
29. Newport News
30. Buck Roe
31. Yeardley's Plantation
32. Savage Neck
33. Wilcox's Plantation
34. Smith's Island

now came to Virginia to save more of his son's countrymen. Thorpe strictly taught Christianity and English mores to the Powhatans. Relationships with many Powhatans placed him as a mediator between the leaders at Jamestown and Chief Opechancanough who frequented Thorpe's college.

In this same period Yeardley negotiated with Opechancanough to allow more openness between the English and Powhatans if the Powhatans supplied more corn. Francis Wyatt arrived as the new governor in November 1621. Wyatt and Thorpe fully embraced Yeardley's deal to enable increased growth of tobacco, sassafras, and the religious conversion of the tribes. Opechancanough then encouraged Powhatans to live and work alongside the English. Wyatt and Thorpe believed they ushered in an age of peace and cohabitation, which the long-time defender of English colonialism, Richard Hakluyt, had promised decades earlier.

Opechancanough was not the Mamanatowick, but he negotiated much more actively than Opitchapam. Opechancanough so frequented English areas that when he changed his name to Mangopeesomon, the English quickly reverted to it and thought nothing of it. Historians now see the moment of the name change as the watershed toward violence. Powhatan culture believed in new names for an accomplished great deed or to summon the goal one wished to pursue. What great deed had Opechancanough accomplished in 1621? Perhaps he reinvigorated Powhatan culture and alliances, but the goal of returning to war to drive the English once again into the sea appears more likely. The year 1622 came into view as religious leaders opened literal doors to Powhatans when they professed interest in Christianity, governmental leaders enabled daily trade of weapons for corn, and the English developed a habit of complacency.

Much scholarship has dug into the connection of Paquiquineo and Opechancanough. If they are the same person, 1622 represents the third cycle in Opechancanough's life of feigned alliance followed by complex ambush. In 1571, Paquiquineo returned to Chesapeake lands with the Catholic priests. At an appointed moment, he and many others simultaneously slew the priests and tore down the mission brick by brick. In the winter of 1609, Smith departed, and a simultaneous revolt destroyed all but two English settlements, driving the English into the sea for a few hours by June. In 1622, Opechancanough masterminded another simultaneous attack, attempting to destroy the English presence. In 1644, the fourth and final cycle of feigned peace and simultaneous ambush struck the English settlements, commanded again by Opechancanough. Four cycles of similar violence lend credence to the first-hand accounts which claimed Opechancanough was over 100 years old when the English captured him in 1646.

In John Smith's *Generall Historie*, he identifies several earlier events as warning signs for the 1622 attack. Smith explains how eastern shore tribes revealed a plot to attack the English in the spring of 1621. Receiving word of this, Yeardley negotiated directly with Opechancanough. Yeardley's fears were relieved when Opechancanough swore that, "the sky should sooner fall than peace be broken." Yeardley, Francis, Thorpe, and many other experienced English colonists believed the colony remained at peace. Smith then describes how a Powhatan war chief, Nemattanew (likely war chief alongside Chief Powhatan's son Parahunt at Powhatan town), lured an Englishman away and killed him on March 12, 1622. Nemattanew's arrogance brought him back to the homestead where servants of the missing man captured and killed him. This strange encounter worried both Governor Wyatt and Opechancanough.

Wyatt sent a letter to Opechancanough apologizing, fearing that the killing of a high-ranking war chief could be bad for relations, but Opechancanough accepted the apology and seemed unfazed. Wyatt's sudden fear of tensions put Opechancanough's plan at risk. Likely, war chief Nemattanew had grown overconfident knowing that hundreds of warriors were already staging for a major assault. Chief Opechancanough, now Mangopeesomon, pressured by the English population, land claims, and religious conversions struck back to clear the land of the invaders.

MASSACRE, FRIDAY MARCH 22, 1622

Opechancanough, as war-chief-of-war-chiefs, coordinated nine tribes to simultaneously attack at eight o'clock in the morning, across a 50-mile stretch of the James River. As many as 1,400 warriors may have participated. On March 21, Powhatan men appeared everywhere; so many that accounts say that Englishmen began loaning out boats to help them cross rivers. The large groups of men brought trading supplies but no weapons. The lack of weapons coaxed the English into inaction assuming the sudden influx needed trade goods. No warnings could spread from town to town because every town saw simultaneous action, with few exceptions. In the words of John Smith:

> … as at other times they came unarmed into our houses, with Deere, Turkies, Fish, Fruits, and other provisions to sell us, yea in some places sat downe at breakfast with our people, whom immediatly with their owne tooles they slew most barbarously, not sparing either age or sex, man woman or childe, so sudden in their execution, that few or none discerned the weapon or blow that brought them to destruction.

Sitting at the breakfast table, working in a field, preaching Christianity, the activity did not matter; at the assigned moment, the warriors of nine tribes killed Englishmen. Some whom the Powhatans knew as friends and some who served as household servants or slaves – all received a sudden and brutal attack.

The Virginia colony in 1622 divided into four "corporations:" Henrico, Charles City, James City, and Elizabeth City. Henrico stretched from the falls of the James to the mouth of the Appomattox River; Charles extended from the mouth of the Appomattox to the mouth of the Chickahominy River; James managed from the Chickahominy River to the Nansemond River, with Elizabeth as the easternmost two capes of the James River. These four corporations helped manage the growing populations living within each. Jamestown, Charles (Bermuda) City, Henrico Fort, and Elizabeth City each acted as the capital or hub for the region. The many first-hand accounts of the attack can be categorized north to south by the corporation they were in. The following pages will discuss the attacks at many of these locations.

The Attacks

Located 60 river miles from Jamestown lay five settlements of the Henrico region: the Falling Creek Ironworks, the Indian College Lands, Sheffield's Plantation, Proctor's Plantation, and Henrico Fort. The Virginia Company greatly valued the Indian College and the Ironworks as two pet projects created directly from London orders. Sheffield and Proctor grew large wheat crops to supply English settlement to the south.

At the ironworks on Falling Creek the morning of March 22, several gentlemen and skilled laborers found themselves trapped by attackers. In all, 21 men, two women, and three children died that morning, from John Berkeley, heir to Beverstone Castle of Gloucestershire, to Collins, an enslaved laborer. No one present survived to tell the story of the events which destroyed the first ironworks in Virginia. Opechancanough had learned from the English examples in the last war, ensuring that, in the 1622 attack, property and resources were destroyed at each location.

The Virginia Company invested in rhetoric and excitement for the future work of the Indian College far up the James River. George Thorpe befriended many Powhatans during his few months as religious leader of the project. Despite many Powhatans feigning interest in the Christian God, the college and 17 servants working its 1,000 acres perished that Friday morning; none survived to tell of the attack.

Sheffield's Plantation and Henrico Fort also saw complete destruction where another 18 men, women, and children perished. But Proctor's Plantation stood as the lone settlement of Henrico to survive. Alice Proctor, John Proctor's wife, gathered her indentured servants and fought off the attackers. Alice Proctor and her men fought defensively from the Proctor blockhouse until rescued by a company of militia, bringing orders for all survivors to evacuate to Jamestown or Flowerdew. Upon her evacuation the awaiting warriors burned the Proctor Plantation.

The Corporation of Charles City contained 19 settlements all attacked that Friday morning. The settlements of Charles City received the same treatment as Henrico with every structure and resource being burned or killed. The more populated settlements lost 142 men, women, and children. The proximity to local tribes increased the attacking warrior numbers well beyond the multiple settlements' capabilities for defense, even if they had had warning. Most of the settlements within the corporation were smaller homesteads with families and few defenses. George Thorpe, the leader of the Indian College, was visiting Berkeley's Hundred that morning. He received early warning from friendly Powhatan converts that an attack on his life was coming. He thought they meant an assassin which he boldly dismissed, believing his divine missionary work would protect him. Ironically, George Thorpe died in a similar manner as Father Segura had in 1572, as the prime target representing acculturation and religious power. Many of the dead at Berkeley's Hundred were mutilated and hacked to pieces. Several of the plantations downriver from Henrico were owned by "ancient planters," men who had endured since the John Smith era. Captain Powell, a veteran from the Dutch wars and of the last Powhatan War, died alongside his family, their heads removed. Nathaniel Causey, a Virginian since 1608, fell to the ground with a hatchet wound at his plantation Causey's Care, but he turned and wrestled the hatchet from his attacker, killing him and driving off others. At Spelman's, Ward's, Maycock's, and several others, Powhatan warriors wiped out whole families and their tenants and servants. The settlement Martin's Brandon, despite a reputation for harboring rough men who committed crimes in Jamestown, saw its population wiped out.

The James City region contained the oldest and best-established settlements. Many homesteads still lacked defenses, but the populations tended to be

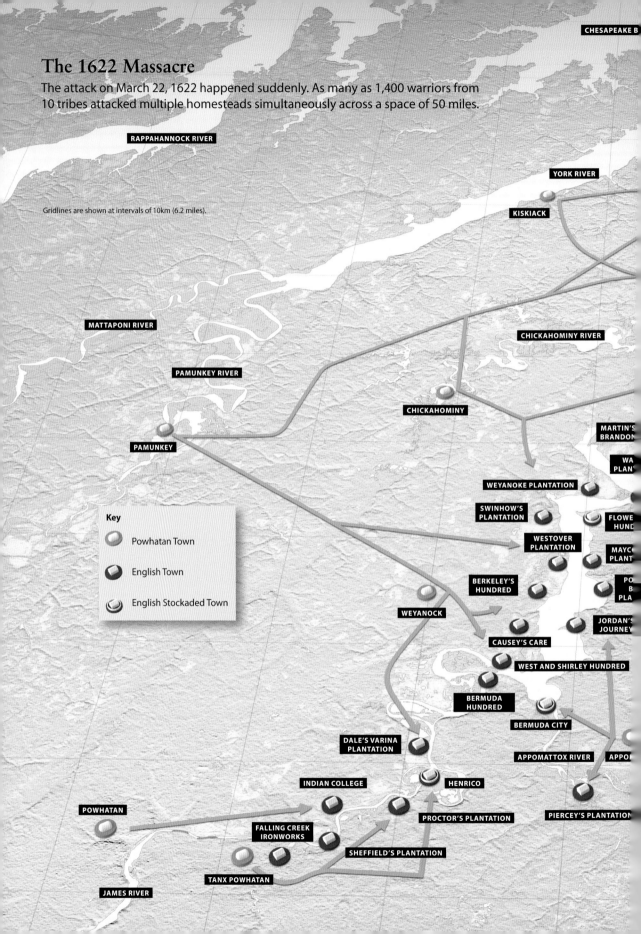

The 1622 Massacre

The attack on March 22, 1622 happened suddenly. As many as 1,400 warriors from 10 tribes attacked multiple homesteads simultaneously across a space of 50 miles.

CHESAPEAKE B

RAPPAHANNOCK RIVER

YORK RIVER

KISKIACK

Gridlines are shown at intervals of 10km (6.2 miles).

MATTAPONI RIVER

CHICKAHOMINY RIVER

PAMUNKEY RIVER

CHICKAHOMINY

MARTIN'S
BRANDON

PAMUNKEY

WA
PLAN

WEYANOKE PLANTATION

SWINHOW'S
PLANTATION

FLOWE
HUND

WESTOVER
PLANTATION

MAYC
PLANT

Key

🔵 Powhatan Town

🔴 English Town

⚪ English Stockaded Town

BERKELEY'S
HUNDRED

PO
B
PLA

WEYANOCK

JORDAN'S
JOURNEY

CAUSEY'S CARE

WEST AND SHIRLEY HUNDRED

BERMUDA
HUNDRED

BERMUDA CITY

DALE'S VARINA
PLANTATION

APPOMATTOX RIVER

APPO

INDIAN COLLEGE

HENRICO

POWHATAN

PROCTOR'S PLANTATION

PIERCEY'S PLANTATION

FALLING CREEK
IRONWORKS

SHEFFIELD'S PLANTATION

TANX POWHATAN

JAMES RIVER

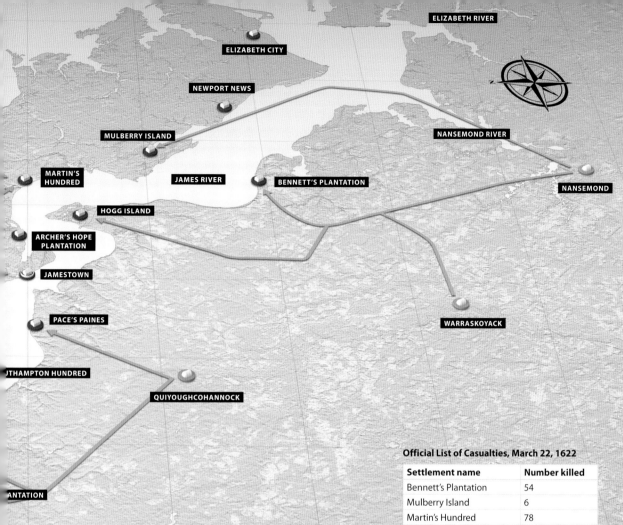

ELIZABETH RIVER

ELIZABETH CITY

NEWPORT NEWS

NANSEMOND RIVER

MULBERRY ISLAND

MARTIN'S HUNDRED

JAMES RIVER

BENNETT'S PLANTATION

NANSEMOND

HOGG ISLAND

ARCHER'S HOPE PLANTATION

JAMESTOWN

WARRASKOYACK

PACE'S PAINES

JTHAMPTON HUNDRED

QUIYOUGHCOHANNOCK

ANTATION

Official List of Casualties, March 22, 1622

Settlement name	Number killed
Bennett's Plantation	54
Mulberry Island	6
Martin's Hundred	78
Hogg Island	5
Archer's Hope Plantation	5
Pace's Paines	5
Southampton Hundred	5
Martin's Brandon	7
Weyanoke Plantation	21
Ward's Plantation	7
Spelman's Plantation	2
Swinhow's Plantation	9
Flowerdew Hundred	6
Westover Plantation	28
Maycock's Plantation	4
Powell's Brook Plantation	12
Berkeley's Hundred	11
Bermuda Hundred	9
Piercey's Plantation	4
Dale's Varina Plantation	8
Henrico	5
Proctor's Plantation	5
Indian College	17
Sheffield's Plantation	13
Falling Creek Ironworks	21
Total	347

Settlements after March 22, 1622

Abandoned	Ordered to become fortified	Damaged but restored	Unaffected in 1622
Berkeley's Hundred	Jamestown and suburbs	Indian College	Jamestown
Southampton Hundred	Newport News	Bermuda City	Elizabeth City
Maycock's Plantation	Elizabeth City	Piercey's Plantation	Newport News
Powell's Brook Plantation	Flowerdew Hundred	Archer's Hope Plantation	Eastern shore
Spelman's Plantation	West and Shirley Hundred	Hogg Island	
Weyanoke Plantation	Jordan's Journey	Martin's Hundred	
		Mulberry Island	
		Bennett's Plantation	

long-term residents. Perhaps the older residents demonstrated more vigilance in self-defense, but more likely the south side of the James River saw attacks from the weakened Nansemonds and Warraskoyacks while the northern side of the river faced the elite Pamunkey and Chickahominy warriors. Many of the south bank settlements of James City drove off their attackers, including several around Bennett's Plantation. James Bennett and his sons fought off warriors at their plantation. A Master Baldwin protected his injured wife, firing his musket over her body many times, "saving her, his house, himself, and diverse others." Captain Rolfe Hamar returned that morning from hunting to find his home burning. He gathered a party of men and counterattacked. Rolfe went to his father Thomas's house to check on the property and found him barricaded inside with warriors around the house. But "Harrison's boy" found his master's gun and began firing from a window to drive the warriors back. Rolfe liberated his father and the boy. A small boat of six musketeers came down from Jamestown to help, but finding every other home burning they evacuated Hamar and 40 people up the river to Jamestown. Even though many fought back along the south side of the river, the loss of property remained extensive and the loss of life records 54 lost.

Jamestown, the capital of the colony, and long-time seat of a five-sided fort with three cannon mounts, posed a looming obstacle to Opechancanough's warriors. J. Frederick Fausz, a premier Jamestown historian, believes that Opechancanough would have reserved his most elite Pamunkey warriors for the assault on Jamestown. But Jamestown was on the alert and the attack never came. On the night of March 21, a Warraskoyack boy named Chanco lay on his sleeping mats talking with his brother inside Pace's Paines Plantation. Chanco confessed to his brother that, as a Christian, he felt it was wrong to kill Mr Perry and Master Pace who had treated him like a son. Chanco and his friend rose from bed and warned Master Pace about the upcoming attack. Pace sent messengers across the river to Jamestown before sunrise. By eight in the morning Jamestown's garrison fully defended the walls. Opechancanough's warriors likely saw the walls bristling with men and the cannoneers on the bulwarks and decided to hit a weaker target.

Martin's Hundred

The presumed shift of warriors away from Jamestown brought an entire army of perhaps 300 onto Martin's Hundred, just seven miles east of Jamestown. The 80,000-acre plantation of Martin's Hundred stood as an exemplary model the Virginia Company hoped to replicate. In 1618, Sir John Wolstenholme, a proud patron of English exploration, sent 220 settlers as the new tenants for his patent south of Jamestown. The settlers built the fortified town of Wolstenholme as the administrative capital for the plantation. Three miles of river-front property placed homesteads along the water's edge. Each home stood some distance from the last, preventing the settlers of Martin's Hundred from supporting one another. The attack of 1622 saw the death of 78 settlers and the capture of 16 women. Martin's Hundred saw the most death and destruction of all locations in the 1622 attack. The enlarged war parties overcame the defenses and burned hundreds of structures at Martin's Hundred.

Martin's Hundred was well fortified and manned. The complete destruction of the settlement demonstrated the surprise and strength of the attackers. This photo is of the recreation of portions of the fort based on Ivor Noël Hume's archeology. (Paul Jones/Alamy Stock Photo)

In the 1970s, archeologist Ivor Noël Hume began a complete survey and intensive excavation of the site. Unbeknown to the archeologists, many remnants of the ancient plantation remained. The plantation was resettled several years after 1622 but the history of death there seemed to have inspired future residents to build their homes and barns away from the traditional sites destroyed in 1622. This enabled the archeologist to uncover with amazing accuracy the former plantation destroyed over 400 years earlier. During Noël Hume's explorations he found the exact post holes for each of the fortified settlements; the burned remains of collapsed structures dated to 1622; armor in the bottom of a filled-in well; human remains laid in grouped graves adjacent to burned structures; and even burned debris inside graves. The extreme accuracy of Noël Hume's archeology has revealed the reality of the attack of March 1622.

An infamous woodcut that saw production across Britain for a generation. The surprise attack of 1622 shocked Christian missionaries and English planners who thought Jamestown verged on religious conversion of the Powhatan. This depiction incorrectly shows Jamestown under attack but helps the viewer understand the horror of the attacks that destroyed many settlements. (Courtesy of the John Carter Brown Library)

According to archeology, 140 people lived around Martin's Hundred in 1621. Several bones and burial sites were found immediately adjacent to structures, implying that the people were killed inside the building or at its doorstep and hastily buried. Several of the skeletal remains showed evidence of dismemberment which is supported by John Smith's and Edward Waterhouse's accounts. Edward Waterhouse wrote the official Virginia Company report on the 1622 Massacre, titled "A Declaration of the state of the Colonie and Affaires in Virginia." The several separated homesites with grouped remains support the traditional narrative of warriors sitting down to breakfast or sleeping in the homes the previous night. Burials discovered perfectly perpendicular to a contemporary fence line indicate the gravedigger followed the fence line to bury the dead.

The aftermath of the 1622 Massacre left more than 347 dead; many of the accounts that list names include wives and children on the same line. These deaths were counted as one, even though some of the lines include one or more children. Rounding up to 400 casualties captures most of the missing names and transcription errors. Four councilmen of the colony were included in the death count: John Thorpe, John Berkeley, Nathaniel Powell, and Samuel Maycock. No Powhatan warriors attacked the Elizabeth City corporation. This leads historians to believe Opechancanough's plan was to destroy all the upriver settlements then besiege Newport News and Elizabeth City as Chief Powhatan did in 1609 and 1610 with Jamestown Island. The attack stunned the English world. The survivors of the colony wrote to London distraught and begging for aid. The abandonment of the many settlements, complete destruction of food supplies, and the inability to plant tobacco or corn in the spring of 1622 spelled a looming disaster and poverty for the Virginians and the Company.

1622, English Counterattack

In London, planners declared "it would be a sin against the dead to abandon the enterprise," and John Smith stated it was "good for the Plantation because now we have just cause to destroy them by all meanes possible." The surprise murder spurred all parties toward revenge and complete destruction of the Powhatan Confederacy. Just as in 1611, the English would make no distinction between formerly friendly or hostile tribes; any who stood in their way were liable to be attacked.

Governor Wyatt announced throughout the colony that all survivors must fortify themselves in defensible strongpoints as they developed a campaign to retaliate. King James I released 1,000 halberds, hundreds of mail shirts, old muskets, and 2,000 iron helmets from the tower of London to be sent directly to Jamestown. The Virginia Company instructed Wyatt to distribute spoils of war among the militias to encourage participation. Wyatt wrote to London, explaining how his first order of business was to move about the country again because Powhatan raiding parties harried any English group attempting travel. By September, Wyatt had readied 300 of his best soldiers. Wyatt commissioned George Yeardley as the field commander and dispatched him to the south side of the James River. Yeardley led 300 soldiers first to the Nansemond towns. Upon their approach, all fled before them. The English burned the towns and planned to harvest the corn but found the Nansemonds had already harvested it and hidden it from them. Yeardley knew the colony lacked food, so they stayed in the area to look for the corn. They crossed the river to quarter at Elizabeth City.

From Elizabeth City, Yeardley felt confident and sailed his army of 300 men up the Pamunkey River, directly to the Pamunkey town. Chief Opechancanough's stronghold refused to meet Yeardley in battle; instead the tribe attempted to negotiate. Promising to bring more corn, the Pamunkey tribe began transporting storehouses of corn away from the town. After waiting 12 days Yeardley realized the scheme and burned the town. While his soldiers burned the houses Pamunkey warriors discharged firearms into his men. The Pamunkey warriors refused open battle but now used European muskets against the Virginian Army. Yeardley left with only a few wounded but had captured "three bushels per man," meaning 900 bushels of corn for the colony. Ending the year 1622, war casualties remained few, but the coming winter held hunger for all.

1623 AND 1624, ENGLISH COUNTERATTACKS

After a decade of peace and sustainability, Jamestown in the early days of 1623 looked much as it had in its early troubling years. Planters had focused their crops on tobacco and sassafras, ignoring corn which could easily be traded with neighboring tribes. With no trading partners, no storehouses, and continual settler arrivals at the ports of Jamestown and Elizabeth City, the population of Virginia plummeted. Accounts say the dead from disease and starvation piled up in the streets of Jamestown until the hogs started eating them. Many letters arrived in England begging for family members to buy out the contracts of indentured servants so they could escape. Almost 400 settlers had died in the March massacre but another 367 are recorded as dying from starvation and disease between April 1622 and February 16, 1623. In one year, the population of Jamestown lost 800 people. A constant influx of vessels maintained the overall population at around 1,200 souls. In 1622, Governor Wyatt made one change from the 1609 troubles and ended the loose hierarchy of militia officers and created new "borough commanders." As of 1623, Wyatt entered the year with intentional borough commanders who had subordinate officers assigned at each occupied plantation. This method resembled the traditional English militia.

Chief Itoyatin (Opitchapam), Mamanatowick of the confederacy, sent emissaries to Wyatt, requesting to plant corn near the Pamunkey villages and promising to deliver captives taken from Martin's Hundred as good will. The request is strange. Itoyatin assumed the English wanted to occupy Pamunkey, but Wyatt accepted the offer because he saw no downside. He now knew the location of a fresh cornfield and Alice Boyse, a prominent English daughter, was delivered as a returned captive to Jamestown. Before Wyatt could devise his next move, Itoyatin again reached out and offered to hold a negotiation at the town of the Patawomeck, where he would deliver the rest of the captives and even offer his brother Opechancanough as a prisoner. After the successful raids the previous fall, Wyatt boldly sent Captain William Tucker with 12 musketeers to negotiate with Itoyatin.

Tucker arrived at the neutral site and reported that 200 Powhatan chiefs had gathered in the village. Despite Wyatt's assumption that it was a trap, Itoyatin seems to have convened an honest meeting hoping to stop the cycle of violence before more English or Powhatans starved. Perhaps Itoyatin as the Mamanatowick was satisfied to keep the English at Jamestown and Elizabeth City. The fact that Opechancanough was present and unarmed shows that he too obeyed the Mamanatowick. Perhaps Opechancanough's ambush had not been as successful as he had boasted and Itoyatin regained influence over the confederacy. All these hypotheses do not mean much because at the meeting Captain Tucker poisoned the wine. Dozens of chiefs immediately reacted and started falling ill. Tucker and his men withdrew and fired into the amassed crowds. Tucker fled back to Jamestown reporting that many "Indian kings and commanders," including Opechancanough, were slain.

Elated by the deaths of the many chiefs Wyatt went on the offensive. In the summer of 1623, Wyatt deployed Captains Peirce, West, Mathews, Tucker, and Maddison against the tribes of the south bank and up the upper James and Chickahominy rivers. Little is known about the engagements, but each raid burned homes and cut down corn to starve the Powhatans in the coming winter. "Wyatt reported to the company that the Powhatans, as expected, had planted corn 'in great abundance, upon hope of a fraudulent peace,'" and that the July raids ravished tribal lands and populations. These successful raids demonstrate that despite being under civilian governance since 1619, Governor Wyatt successfully transferred the administration to a war footing. Also, in the summer of 1623 he drafted every twentieth man to build a fort on the south side of the river and he ordered corn planted at every homestead. In November, Wyatt again assembled his captains. Captains Maddison, Tucker, and Whitaker represented a militia of 90 men whom Wyatt personally led all the way up the Potomac River. This large raiding party attacked the Pascoticon tribe, a tribe not allied or connected with the Powhatan Confederacy. Using his moment of strength, Wyatt started extending dominance over more tribes of the Chesapeake and brought the Patawomecks back into alliance with Jamestown. The long-distance raid encouraged the non-aligned Patawomecks to formally rejoin with the English. At the end of 1623, Wyatt had embarrassed Itoyatin and restored a critical trading partner for the English.

The Virginia House of Burgesses passed a law in the spring of 1624 that all homesteads be palisaded, all men must carry on their person a weapon,

Second Anglo-Powhatan War: Events of 1622–24

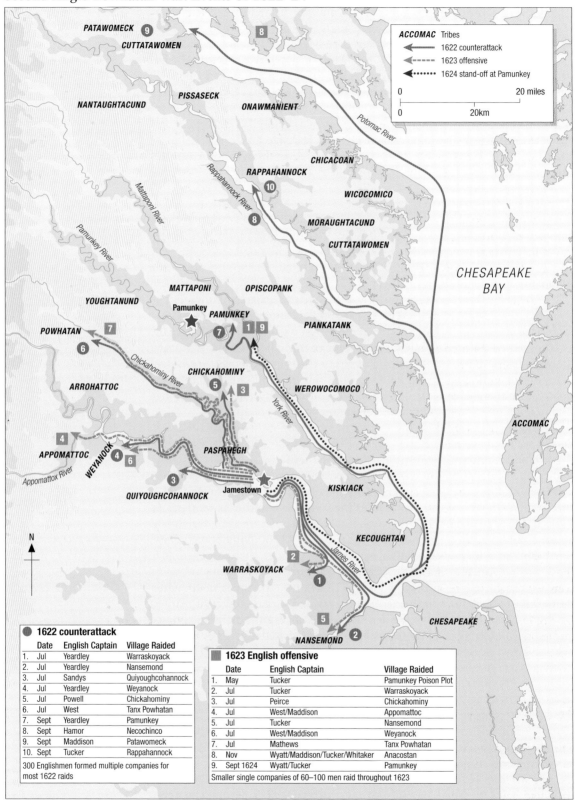

ACCOMAC Tribes

→ 1622 counterattack

→ 1623 offensive

→ 1624 stand-off at Pamunkey

0		20 miles
0	20km	

CHESAPEAKE BAY

PATAWOMECK ⑨
CUTTATAWOMEN
⑧ (8)
PISSASECK
NANTAUGHTACUND
ONAWMANIENT
Potomac River
CHICACOAN
RAPPAHANNOCK
⑩
WICOCOMICO
Rappahannock River
Mattaponi River
⑧ (8)
MORAUGHTACUND
CUTTATAWOMEN
Pamunkey River
MATTAPONI
OPISCOPANK
YOUGHTANUND
Pamunkey ★ PAMUNKEY
PIANKATANK
⑦ [7]
POWHATAN [7] ① ⑨
⑥
Chickahominy River
ARROHATTOC
CHICKAHOMINY
⑤
[3]
WEROWOCOMOCO
York River
ACCOMAC
[4]
WEYANOCK
[4] [6]
APPOMATTOC
PASPAHEGH
Appomattox River
[3]
KISKIACK
Jamestown ★
QUIYOUGHCOHANNOCK
KECOUGHTAN
N
James River
[2]
①
WARRASKOYACK
[5]
②
CHESAPEAKE
NANSEMOND

● 1622 counterattack

	Date	English Captain	Village Raided
1.	Jul	Yeardley	Warraskoyack
2.	Jul	Yeardley	Nansemond
3.	Jul	Sandys	Quiyoughcohannock
4.	Jul	Yeardley	Weyanock
5.	Jul	Powell	Chickahominy
6.	Jul	West	Tanx Powhatan
7.	Sept	Yeardley	Pamunkey
8.	Sept	Hamor	Necochinco
9.	Sept	Maddison	Patawomeck
10.	Sept	Tucker	Rappahannock

300 Englishmen formed multiple companies for most 1622 raids

▨ 1623 English offensive

	Date	English Captain	Village Raided
1.	May	Tucker	Pamunkey Poison Plot
2.	Jul	Tucker	Warraskoyack
3.	Jul	Peirce	Chickahominy
4.	Jul	West/Maddison	Appomattoc
5.	Jul	Tucker	Nansemond
6.	Jul	West/Maddison	Weyanock
7.	Jul	Mathews	Tanx Powhatan
8.	Nov	Wyatt/Maddison/Tucker/Whitaker	Anacostan
9.	Sept 1624	Wyatt/Tucker	Pamunkey

Smaller single companies of 60–100 men raid throughout 1623

and required the regulation of gunpowder to prevent its purchase by Native Americans. Wyatt developed a campaign schedule or "marches" to bi-annually raid the Powhatans. In June, there was a raid intended to cut down growing corn, then in November the second raid was intended to steal any unharvested corn and burn down the rest, causing famine in January and February for the chosen tribe. Summer 1624 saw Francis Wyatt's greatest victory. Chief Mangopeesomon (Opechancanough) remained hidden and presumably ill since the poisoning incident, leaving Chief Itoyatin as the premier leader of the confederacy. Itoyatin sent messengers north to tribes above the Potomac River, trying to capitalize on the destruction the English had meted out on them, telling them that the Powhatans would feed all who allied with them and when the foreigners came for their corn that year, the battle would be remembered for all time.

Francis Wyatt unknowingly obliged Chief Itoyatin's boasts. By 1624, Wyatt's large 300-man militia from 1622 was uninterested in long-range combat. Instead, Wyatt brought 60 fully armored musketeers to raid the Pamunkey village. Wyatt did not intend to fight the entire Powhatan army; he intended to cut down the growing corn and run, but upon arrival 800 Powhatan warriors with a core of Pamunkey bowmen opposed Wyatt's landing on the shores of Pamunkey. Several visiting chiefs from the north watched the battle unfold. Wyatt marched his men north toward the rolling cornfields spreading across the lowlands of the Pamunkey River. He dispatched 24 men to begin cutting as much corn as they could while 36 musketeers remained in reserve to delay the massive Powhatan army. Standing in rank and file the musketeers fired their English snaphance muskets. A snaphance is not a simple weapon yet Wyatt's men performed well, firing volleys in ranks to great effect against the Powhatan bowmen.

The musketeers fired until the Powhatan arrows and formation forced them away, but the team of two dozen cutters had cut tens of acres. Wyatt called for an orderly withdrawal downriver, where they hid waiting to reattack the next day. Day two of the great battle at Pamunkey played out much the same. A team of cutters ran for the vast Pamunkey fields, and a small company of men fired volleys as long as they could. The musketeers fired so well the Pamunkeys gave up their attempt to engage the cutting teams and waited near the village to prevent its destruction. Little did the Powhatan force know but the musketeers had run low on ammunition. The musketeers stood as a blocking force while hundreds of remaining warriors watched the cutting team destroy and set fire to the Pamunkey fields. After destroying enough corn to feed 4,000 people for a year, Wyatt withdrew, having lost 16 men to Powhatan arrows but crushing the Powhatan morale and reputation in front of the assembled allies and potential allies that had observed the battle. Upon Wyatt's return to Jamestown, he wrote a letter to London asking for more gunpower as they had expended it all during 1624.

1624–34, SEPARATE SPHERES

The English respected the Powhatans for facing them in open battle. The set-piece battle demonstrated to both sides that the other still had strength. Despite many raids and destruction of property and homes, no Powhatan tribe had been destroyed or driven away. Similarly, the continuous flow of

Attack on Pamunkey, 1624 (PP. 84–85)

By 1624, English soldiers at Jamestown relied almost exclusively on muskets, bringing the latest snaphance variant to Virginia (**1**). Officers and noblemen in the early 17th century wore plate armor and such examples (**2**) have been recovered in archeological digs at Jamestown.

During this attack, Chief Itoyatin hoped to mass his warriors as a show of force against the English. 800 Powhatan warriors (**3**), of many tribes but mainly Pamunkey, engaged the English soldiers with arrow volleys. Arrows fell and wounded the Englishmen despite their heavy European armor (**4**). In return, 36 musketeers formed three ranks to fire continuously on the Pamunkey warriors while 24 more Englishmen formed teams to systematically burn the nearby cornfields (**5**). The constant barrage from musketeers prevented the massed warriors from approaching the small English formation.

After the conflict, Jamestown leaders wrote to London desperately asking for more powder after expending a majority of the colony's supply during the battle. In 1624, the Pamunkey village site represented the largest population (**6**) of Powhatan peoples, surrounded by acres of corn. The burning of the cornfields weakened the confederacy's influence over allied tribes. Chief Itoyatin's inability to defeat the small English force in open combat discredited him and reestablished Opechancaough as the leading Powhatan chief. After this battle, Powhatan war chiefs remained on the defensive as English seasonal raids repeatedly disrupted food production and Powhatan alliances.

settlers repopulated the Virginia settlements. Once again, no side possessed the strength to destroy the other. By the end of 1624, London planners had had enough of complaints and desperate pleas for food and ammunition and no profits to show for it. The king revoked the company charter and personally assumed control of the colony. Unfortunately, or fortunately, for the Virginia colony King James I passed away, passing the throne to Charles I. Charles focused his efforts elsewhere for much of the 1620s, leaving the Virginia colony still to its own devices. The lack of gunpowder prevented any English raids in 1625 and there are no records of military activities in 1626. The colony transitioned to a strong defense, improving and building more fortified positions across the region.

With a resupply of gunpowder in 1627, Wyatt's bi-annual plan for marches took effect, seeing the Virginians conduct the same pattern of raids across the south side of the James River, then up the Powhatan and Chickahominy rivers, culminating in a raid on Pamunkey. Each small-scale raid and counter-raid tested and tried Powhatan and English wills. In 1628, Royal Governor Francis West arrived to manage the colony. Wyatt's last act established a plan to build a palisade wall to separate the English from the Powhatans. Governor West enacted the plan by sending Captain William Claiborne to destroy the Kiskiack on the south end of the Pamunkey River. Claiborne attacked and drove them out in summer 1630. At this time Jamestown received word that Chief Mangopeesomon had ascended as the Mamanatowick. The English feared their long-time nemesis now leading the confederacy would ramp up violence again. But Opechancanough/Mangopeesomon at 90 years old was seen visiting other tribes carried on a litter surrounded by dozens of warriors. The great and ancient chief did not seem interested in violence and offered peace to the English.

Royal Governor John Harvey hesitantly accepted the peace offer in 1632 but added a decree to all English settlements forbidding Native Americans from entering their property unless they had a direct message from the great king. Another decade of violence and raids ended with wary peace and two cultures who believed the less they saw of each other the better life could be. Small-scale raids and killing still occurred on both sides, but overall, the colony and the confederacy moved into a new decade of peace. With the Kiskiack removed the English built a four-mile-long wall across the Virginia Peninsula. From Archer's Hope Creek (modern-day College Creek) to Queen's Creek, a wall barricaded 300,000 acres from Powhatan incursion. The wall did not define the farthest extent of English power, but it established the inner ring, the citadel of the growing English Empire. The Great Palisade was completed in 1634 after the major hostilities of the Second Anglo-Powhatan War. The wall, less formidable than advertised, did create a clear barrier defining English Christian soil from the mixed borderland frontier and distant Powhatan strongholds. The dreams of empire which began under Queen Elizabeth I developed into a resilient colony in the New World supported by a network of overseas holdings: Bermuda in 1612, Massachusetts in 1620/30, St Kitts in 1624, Barbados in 1627, Maryland in 1632, and Rhode Island in 1636. Jamestown and its citadel of the Virginia Peninsula, forged through starvation, deprivation, and bloodshed, remained a foundation for Britain's overseas empire.

AFTERMATH

The Virginia colony represented an amalgamation of the many types of overseas experiments conducted by early English leaders. Jamestown experimented with conquest, trade, mineral exploitation, labor exploitation, and ended with a balance of planting and trade. After the Second Anglo-Powhatan War, the settlers of Virginia would have one last major clash with the Powhatan Confederacy in 1644–46. After the 1624 great battle at Pamunkey, the Powhatan Confederacy began a long decline in the face of English growth. In the late 1620s the balance of power in the Chesapeake could have fallen in either direction given a few changes of fate. Francis Wyatt capitalized on his talents of administration, thereby keeping the colony alive after 1622. The poisoning of Opechancanough significantly weakened the Powhatan organization, and Itoyatin could not lead in the same way Chief Powhatan and Opechancanough had. Veteran English warriors from around the world brought early modern war to Virginia just in time to overcome traditional Powhatan archery.

By 1644, the English settlements once again outgrew their bounds; settlers and squatters stretched homesteads far from the control of the Virginia Peninsula citadel. Just as during the previous three cycles, Chief Mangopeesomon, previously known as Opechancanough, acted old and weak and lulled the English into apathy toward the Powhatans. Once again Native Americans and Englishmen lived side by side and in one another's houses. Chief Mangopeesomon again coordinated a large-scale ambush to destroy the English in their homes. The initial attack at dawn on April 18, 1644, led to the death of almost 500 settlers. This high cost represented a quarter of the colony's population. Just as in 1622 the settlers regrouped, instead of at Jamestown this time at the middle plantation, which stood as the centerpiece to the Great Palisade across the peninsula. Then they began their furious counterattack against the James River and Pamunkey River tribes who had attacked them. In 1645, the colony halted offensive operations, again due to a shortage of gunpowder. This hiatus came with the added challenge of the ongoing English Civil War. Calls for arrest of Cavaliers or Roundheads echoed across Virginia, but the threat of Powhatan danger refocused the colony. By 1646, the next round of raids captured the Mamanatowick and imprisoned him at Jamestown. The 1646 counter-raids permanently drove away many tribes. The tribes on the south bank migrated farther south into Carolina. Tribes on the York and Potomac rivers moved west. Powhatans in the center fought on until the death of Mangopeesomon in 1646 at the hands of a prison guard. The great chief was said to have been 102 years old.

Third Anglo-Powhatan War: Events of 1644–46

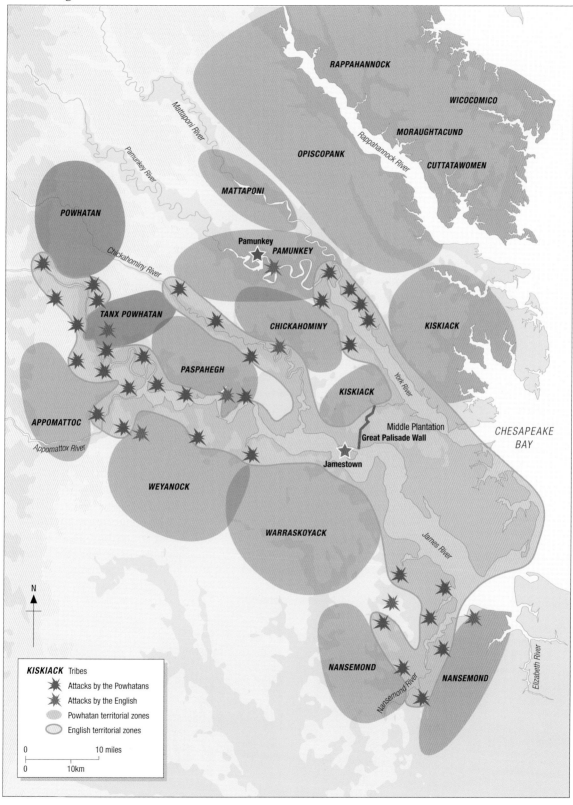

Legend:
- **KISKIACK** Tribes
- Attacks by the Powhatans
- Attacks by the English
- Powhatan territorial zones
- English territorial zones

0 — 10 miles
0 — 10km

Map labels: RAPPAHANNOCK, WICOCOMICO, MORAUGHTACUND, OPISCOPANK, CUTTATAWOMEN, Mattaponi River, Rappahannock River, Pamunkey River, MATTAPONI, POWHATAN, Chickahominy River, Pamunkey, PAMUNKEY, KISKIACK, TANX POWHATAN, CHICKAHOMINY, PASPAHEGH, York River, KISKIACK, APPOMATTOC, Appomattox River, Middle Plantation, Great Palisade Wall, CHESAPEAKE BAY, Jamestown, WEYANOCK, WARRASKOYACK, James River, NANSEMOND, NANSEMOND, Nansemond River, Elizabeth River, N

THE BATTLEFIELD TODAY

The Virginia Department of Historic Resources has helped steward the critical sites of English, Virginian, and American history for two centuries. Many locations of the original Jamestown settlements and the colony of Virginia are well preserved and recorded through the various historical endeavors of government agencies, private conservationists, and university programs.

Today Virginians refer to the "historic triangle," an area which includes Jamestown, Williamsburg, and Yorktown. This region of the state of Virginia contains many museums and preservation operations to explore and protect the history of the region. The fort at Jamestown was thought to have been washed away by erosion on the James River, until 1994, when new archeological surveys found the archeological evidence confirming the fort's location. Since then, a renaissance in Jamestown history has restored many of the lost stories of the earliest days of the Virginia settlement.

The famous spit of land connecting the island to the mainland remains the access point to the island, allowing millions of visitors to drive onto the ancient settlement. Past and ongoing archeology is viewable on the island of Jamestown. A good portion of the fort has been reconstructed and several buildings from the 17th century have recreation timber frames to demonstrate their size and shape. Jamestown Island is registered as a National Historic Site of the United States. Back across the land bridge the Jamestown-Yorktown Foundation manages a fantastic facility: a state-of-the-art museum dedicated to Jamestown and early English colonization and an outdoor area recreating the Jamestown Fort, port, and a Powhatan village. At the port lies the beautiful full-scale replica of the *Susan Constant* from the 1607 expedition.

BELOW LEFT
The site of Jamestown Fort has undergone extensive modern archeology and the reconstruction of many buildings. (Ryan M. Kelly/AFP via Getty Images)

BELOW RIGHT
The Jamestown-Yorktown Foundation provides a living history of Jamestown. (Tim Graham/Getty Images)

Carter's Grove, the 18th-century plantation built over the site of Martin's Hundred, still stands today, preserved and well developed by the work of Ivor Noël Hume. Unfortunately, the site has been closed to visitors and is currently owned by a private organization. Moving up the river, many of the homestead sites grew into new plantations in the 18th and 19th centuries. Most are marked or remembered as a Jamestown settlement. Shirley, Berkeley, Westover, Bermuda City, Varina, Martin's Brandon, and a few others all have reserved land sites dedicated to the historic settlement. The site of Henrico Fort near the mouth of the Appomattoc River is partially preserved. The land is a nature sanctuary and hosts a few reconstructed buildings and living history to teach about the history of Henrico County.

The homelands of the indigenous peoples are much less preserved than the old settlements. Today five tribes of the original Powhatan paramount chiefdom are US federally recognized tribes: the Pamunkey, Chickahominy, East Chickahominy, Mattaponi, and Nansemond. Chief Powhatan's critical homelands have no major historical remembrance or preserved land except the site of Werowocomoco, the religious center in Chief Powhatan's day. The city of Richmond has been built on the Powhatan homeland.

The stronghold of Opechancanough's Pamunkey tribe is a recognized reservation of the tribe. Opechancanough's century of warfare against European invaders paid dividends. The 1646 treaty stipulated that no Native Americans could enter lands between the James and York rivers, but this had a minor effect on the Pamunkey who remained in their ancient homelands on the Pamunkey River's north bank. Today the Pamunkey tribe maintains 1,600 acres of its ancient homeland. A museum to Pamunkey history sits at the heart of their traditional village. The battlefields of Pamunkey and Nansemond are rural or natural areas which have no formal marking of the battles of 1611 or 1624.

Living history replicas at the Jamestown-Yorktown Foundation Museum. (Richard T. Nowitz/Getty Images)

BELOW LEFT
Many elements of the 1980s archeology at Martin's Hundred enabled the creation of basic reconstruction to represent the exact locations of the original buildings abandoned in 1622. (Paul Jones/Alamy Stock Photo)

BELOW RIGHT
Outside the Pamunkey Indian Museum stands a recently installed bust of Chief Powhatan. The legacy of his ancient confederacy survives through the five federally recognized and six state-recognized native tribes of Virginia. (Dennis Tarnay, Jr./ Alamy Stock Photo)

BIBLIOGRAPHY

Primary Sources

Barbour, Philip L., *The Jamestown Voyages Under the First Charter, 1606-1609: Documents Relating to the Foundation of Jamestown and the History of the Jamestown Colony up to the Departure of Captain John Smith, Last President of the Council in Virginia Under the First Charter, Early in October 1609*, published for the Hakluyt Society [by] Cambridge University Press, London, UK (1969)

Nicholls, Mark, "George Percy's 'Trewe Relacyon': A Primary Source for the Jamestown Settlement," *Virginia Historical Society*, 2005, vol. 113, no. 3 (2005), *https://www.jstor.org/stable/4250269*

Percy, George, *Observations gathered out of a Discourse of the Plantation of the Southerne Colonie in Virginia by the English, 1606*, www.virtualjamestown.org/exist/cocoon/jamestown/fha/J1002

Rolfe, John, John Dale, John Cook Wyllie, and Francis L. Berkeley, *A True Relation of the State of Virginia Lefte by Sir Thomas Dale, Knight, In May Last 1616*, Printed for H.C.T. by C.P.R. at the Printing-Office of the Yale University Press, New Haven, CT (1951)

Smith, John, *A True Relation of Such Occurrences and Accidents of Note as Hath Hapned in Virginia Since the First Planting of that Colony, which is now resident in the South part thereof, till the last returne from thence. Written by Captaine Smith one of the said Collony, to a worshipfull friend of his in England*, printed by John Tappe (1608)

Smith, John, William Symonds and Thomas Abbay, *A Map of Virginia: With a Description of the Countrey, the Commodities, People, Government and Religion. Written by Captaine Smith, Sometimes Governour of the Countrey. Whereunto Is Annexed the Proceedings of Those Colonies, Since Their First Departure From England, With the Discourses, Orations, and Relations of the Salvages, and the Accidents That Befell Them In All Their Iournies and Discoveries. Taken Faithfully As They Were Written Out of the Writings of Doctor Russell. Tho. Studley. Anas Todkill. Ieffra Abot. Richard Wiefin. Will. Phettiplace. Nathaniel Povvell. Richard Pots. And the Relations of Divers Other Diligent Observers There Present Then, and Now Many of Them In England*, Joseph Barnes, London (1612)

Smith, John, *The Generall Historie of Virginia, New-England, and the Summer Isles: With the Names of the Adventurers, Planters, and Governours From Their First Beginning. An⁰: 1584. To This Present 1626. With the Procedings of Those Severall Colonies and the Accidents That Befell Them In All Their Journyes and Discoveries. Also the Maps and Descriptions of All Those Countryes, Their Commodities, People, Government, Customes, and Religion Yet Knowne. Divided Into Six Bookes. By Captaine Iohn Smith Sometymes Governour In Those Countryes & Admirall of New England*, I. D. and I. H. for Edward Blackmore, London (1632)

Smith, John, and Philip L. Barbour, *The Complete Works of Captain John Smith (1580–1631)*, Vol. 1–3, published for the Institute of Early American History and Culture, Williamsburg, VA, By the University of North Carolina Press, Chapel Hill, NC (1986)

William Strachey, Louis B. Wright, and Virginia Freund, *The Historie of Travell into Virginia Britannia* (1612), Lessingdruckerei, Wiesbaden, Hakluyt Society (1967)

Tanner, Mathias, Tracy W. McGregor Library, and McGregor Fund, *Societas Jesu Usque Ad Sanguinis Et Vitae Profusionem Militans, In Europa, Africa, Asia, Et America, Contra Gentiles, Mahometanos, Judaeos, Haereticos, Impios, Pro Deo, Fide, Ecclesia, Pietate: Sive Vita, Et Mors Eorum, Qui Ex Societate Jesu In Causa Fidei, & Virtutis Propugnatae, Violentâ Morte Toto Orbe Sublati Sunt*, Typis Universitatis Carolo-Ferdinandeae, in collegio Societatis Jesu ad S. Clementem, per Joannem Nicolaum Hampel Factorem, Pragae (1675)

Secondary Sources: Books

Appelbaum, Robert, and John Wood Sweet, *Envisioning an English Empire: Jamestown and the Making of the North Atlantic World*, University of Pennsylvania Press, Philadelphia, PA (2005)

Axtell, James, "Chapter 10: Rise and Fall of the Powhatan Empire," in *After Columbus: Essays in the Ethnohistory of Colonial North America*, Oxford University Press, New York (1988)

Beverley, Robert, *History and Present State of Virginia*, printed for R. Parker, HeinOnline Religion and the Law, London, UK (1705)

Crutchfield, James A., *Tribute to an Artist: The Jamestown Paintings of Sidney E. King*, Dietz Press, Richmond, VA (2006)

De Groot, Bouko, *Dutch Armies of the 80 Years' War 1568–1648*, Osprey Publishing, Oxford, UK (2017)

Durham, Keith, *Border Reivers 1513–1603*, Osprey Publishing, Oxford, UK (2011)

Egloff, Keith, and Deborah Woodward, *First People the Early Indians of Virginia*, 2nd edn, University of Virginia Press in association with the Virginia Dept. of Historic Resources, Charlottesville, VA (2006)

Fausz, J. Frederick, "The Powhatan Uprising of 1622: A Historical Study of Ethnocentrism and Cultural Conflict," (1977), Dissertations, Theses, and Masters Projects. William & Mary. Paper 1539623701, https://dx.doi.org/doi:10.21220/s2-3s9r-as79

Games, Allison, *Webs of Empire: English Cosmopolitans in an Age of Expansion, 1560–1660*, Oxford University Press, Oxford, UK (2008)

Grenier, John, *The First Way of War: American War Making on the Frontier, 1607–1814*, Cambridge University Press, Cambridge, UK (2005)

Heath, Ian, *The Irish Wars 1485–1603*, Osprey Publishing, Oxford, UK (1993)

Horn, James, *A Land as God Made It: Jamestown and the Birth of America*, Basic Books, New York (2005)

Horn, James, *A Brave and Cunning Prince: The Great Chief Opechancanough and the War for America*, Basic Books, New York (2021)

Jenks, Tudor, *Captain John Smith*, The Century Co., New York (1904)

Johnson, Michael, *American Woodland Indians*, Osprey Publishing, Oxford, UK (1992)

Johnson, Michael, *American Indians of the Southeast*, Osprey Publishing, Oxford, UK (1995)

Kelso, William M., *Kingsmill Plantations, 1619–1800: Archaeology of Country Life in Colonial Virginia*, Academic Press, Orlando, FL (1984)

Konstam, Angus, *Elizabethan Sea Dogs 1560–1605*, Osprey Publishing, Oxford, UK (2000)

Noël Hume, Ivor, *Martin's Hundred*, Alfred A. Knopf, New York (1982)

Roberts, Keith, *Matchlock Musketeer 1588–1688*, Osprey Publishing, Oxford, UK (2002)

Roberts, Keith, *Pike and Shot Tactics 1590–1660*, Osprey Publishing, Oxford, UK (2010)

Rountree, Helen C., *The Powhatan Indians of Virginia: Their Traditional Culture*, University of Oklahoma Press, Norman, OK (1989)

Rountree, Helen C., *Pocahontas, Powhatan, Opechancanough: Three Indian Lives Changed by Jamestown*, University of Virginia Press, Charlottesville, VA (2005)

Rutman, Darrett Bruce, "A Militant New World, 1607–1640: America's First Generation: Its Martial Spirit, Its Tradition of Arms, Its Militia Organization, Its Wars," University of Virginia, Corcoran Department of History, Charlottesville, VA, PHD thesis (1959). doi. org/10.18130/V35W4B

Sams, Conway Whittle, *The Conquest of Virginia: The Forest Primeval: An Account, Based on Original Documents, of the Indians in that Portion of the Continent in Which Was Established the First English Colony in America*, Putnam, New York (1916)

Scarboro, D. Dewey, *Sir Thomas Dale: A Study of the Marshal and Deputy-governor of Virginia*, Thesis (MA) Emory University, 1963, Charlottesville, VA (1963)

Schmidt, Ethan, *The Divided Dominion: Social Conflict and Indian Hatred in Early Virginia*, University Press of Colorado, Boulder, CO (2015)

Williams, Tony, *The Jamestown Experiment: The Remarkable Story of the Enterprising Colony and the Unexpected Results That Shaped America*, Sourcebooks, Naperville, IL (2011)

Winsbro, Nancy Lee, *The Governorships of Sir Thomas West, Lord Delaware, Sir Thomas Gates and Sir Thomas Dale in Virginia, 1610–1616*, Thesis (MA) University of Virginia, Charlottesville, VA (1955)

Woolley, Benjamin, *Savage Kingdom: The True Story of Jamestown, 1607, and the Settlement of America*, HarperCollins Publishers, New York (2007)

Secondary Sources: Articles

Barbour, Philip L., "The Honorable George Percy, Premier Chronicler of the First Virginia Voyage," *Early American Literature* 6, no. 1 (1971): 7–17, http://www.jstor.org/stable/25070496

Bennett, John T., "The Forgotten Genocide in Colonial America: Reexamining the 1622 Jamestown Massacre Within the Framework of the UN Genocide Convention," *Journal of the History of International Law*, vol. 19, no. 1 (January 1, 2017): 1–49

Chapman, Ellen, "Virginia Tribes," Cultural Heritage Partners, https://arcg.is/0ayzm8

Evans, Kasey, "Temperate Revenge: Religion, Profit, and Retaliation in 1622 Jamestown," *Texas Studies in Literature and Language* 54, no. 1 (2012): 155–88, http://www.jstor.org/stable/41349153

Fausz, J. Frederick, "An 'Abundance of Blood Shed on Both Sides': England's First Indian War, 1609–1614," *The Virginia Magazine of History and Biography*, vol. 98, no. 1 (January 1, 1990): 3–56

Fausz, J. Frederick, "A Tale of Two Colonies: What Really Happened in Virginia and Bermuda? Virginia Bernhard," *The Virginia Magazine of History and Biography*, vol. 120, no. 3 (January 1, 2012): 276–79

Games, Alison, "Violence on the Fringes: The Virginia (1622) and Amboyna (1623) Massacres," *History*, vol. 99, no. 336 (July 1, 2014): 505–29

Garrett, W. R., "The Father of Representative Government in America," *The American Historical Magazine*, vol. 1, no. 1 (1896): 3–21, http://www.jstor.org/stable/43700484

Hecht, Irene W. D., "The Virginia Muster of 1624/5 as a Source for Demographic History," *The William and Mary Quarterly*, vol. 30, no. 1 (1973): 65–92, https://doi.org/10.2307/1923703

Levy, Philip, "A New Look at an Old Wall," *Virginia Magazine of History and Biography*, vol. 112, no. 3 (June 1, 2004): 226–65

Mohlmann, Nicholas K., "Making a Massacre: The 1622 Virginia 'massacre,' Violence, and the Virginia Company of London's Corporate Speech," *Early American Studies, An Interdisciplinary Journal*, vol. 19, no. 3, July, 1 2021: 419–56

Noël Hume, Ivor, and Audrey Noël Hume, "The Archaeology of Martin's Hundred: Part 1, Interpretive Studies; Part 2, Artifact Catalog," University of Pennsylvania Press (2001), http://www.jstor.org/stable/j.ctt1d4tznk

Rose, E. M., "Lord Delaware, First Governor of Virginia, 'the Poorest Baron of This Kingdom,'" *Virginia Magazine of History & Biography*, vol. 128, no. 3 (July 1, 2020): 226–58

Rutman, Darrett B., "The Historian and the Marshal: A Note on the Background of Sir Thomas Dale," *The Virginia Magazine of History and Biography*, vol. 68, no. 3 (1960): 284–94, http://www.jstor.org/stable/4246671

Tarter, Brent, "Sir John Harvey," *Virginia Magazine of History & Biography*, vol. 125, no. 1 (January 1, 2017): 3–37

Vaughan, Alden T., "'Expulsion of the Salvages': English Policy and the Virginia Massacre of 1622," *The William and Mary Quarterly*, vol. 35, no. 1 (1978): 57–84, https://doi.org/10.2307/1922571

"The Virginia Census, 1624–25," *The Virginia Magazine of History and Biography*, vol. 7, no. 4 (1900): 364–67

Websites

https://www.chesapeakeconservancy.org/what-we-do/explore/find-your-chesapeake/about-the-trail/

https://encyclopediavirginia.org/

http://www.virtualjamestown.org

https://pamunkey.org/

INDEX